FLOYD CLYMER'S MOTORCYCLIST'S LIBRARY

THE RALEIGH HANDBOOK

A COMPLETE GUIDE FOR OWNERS AND PROSPECTIVE PURCHASERS OF RALEIGH MOTOR-CYCLES

DEALING WITH EVERY PHASE OF MOTOR-CYCLING, FROM THE REGISTRATION TO THE SELLING OF THE MACHINE SECOND-HAND. INCLUDING CHAPTERS ON DRIVING, TOURING, LEGAL MATTERS, INSURANCE, AND OVERHAULING

BY
"MENTOR"

THIRD EDITION
1930

ANNOUNCEMENT

By special arrangement with the original publishers of this book, Sir Isaac Pitman & Son, Ltd., of London, England, we have secured the exclusive publishing rights for this book, as well as all others in THE MOTORCYCLIST'S LIBRARY.

Included in THE MOTORCYCLIST'S LIBRARY are complete instruction manuals covering the care and operation of respective motorcycles and engines; valuable data on speed tuning, and thrilling accounts of motorcycle race events. See listing of available titles elsewhere in this edition.

We consider it a privilege to be able to offer so many fine titles to our customers.

FLOYD CLYMER
Publisher of Books Pertaining to Automobiles and Motorcycles

2125 W. PICO ST.   LOS ANGELES 6, CALIF.

PREFACE

THIS handbook is launched with the intention of being a " guide and faithful friend " to Raleigh owners present and future in particular, and also as a general treatise on the management, overhaul, and simple repair of motor-cycles.

It is obvious that much of the information contained in this book applies to other machines than the Raleigh ; such a matter as carburation, for instance, applies equally well to any make ; but where details of practice differ, only those details applicable to the Raleigh are dealt with.

It is hoped that the hints and tips given throughout the book will be found helpful to the reader ; they are all the result of a very enjoyable and practical experience with various Raleigh motor-cycles—and with other machines in the old days when the Raleigh was not so well known as it is to-day.

The writer would like to take this opportunity of thanking Miss Marjorie Cottle, the well-known amateur competition rider, for the valuable chapter she has kindly written on " Motor-Cycling for Ladies," which will be of great assistance to the ever-growing band of lady motor-cyclists.

It is impossible, in a book of this size, to deal fully with every aspect of the sport of motor-cycling ; should any reader experience any special difficulty, a letter addressed to " Mentor," c/o the Publishers (with a stamped addressed envelope), will bring helpful advice in the course of a post or so.

The writer has pleasure in acknowledging his indebtedness to The Raleigh Cycle Co. Ltd. for much valuable assistance, and for their kindness in having many special photographs taken to illustrate the text.

MENTOR.

INTRODUCTION

Welcome to the world of digital publishing ~ the book you now hold in your hand, while unchanged from the original edition, was printed using the latest state of the art digital technology. The advent of print-on-demand has forever changed the publishing process, never has information been so accessible and it is our hope that this book serves your informational needs for years to come. If this is your first exposure to digital publishing, we hope that you are pleased with the results. Many more titles of interest to the classic automobile and motorcycle enthusiast, collector and restorer are available via our website at www.VelocePress.com. We hope that you find this title as interesting as we do.

NOTE FROM THE PUBLISHER

The information presented is true and complete to the best of our knowledge. All recommendations are made without any guarantees on the part of the author or the publisher, who also disclaim all liability incurred with the use of this information.

TRADEMARKS

We recognize that some words, model names and designations, for example, mentioned herein are the property of the trademark holder. We use them for identification purposes only. This is not an official publication.

INFORMATION ON THE USE OF THIS PUBLICATION

This manual is an invaluable resource for the classic motorcycle enthusiast and a "must have" for owners interested in performing their own maintenance. However, in today's information age we are constantly subject to changes in common practice, new technology, availability of improved materials and increased awareness of chemical toxicity. As such, it is advised that the user consult with an experienced professional prior to undertaking any procedure described herein. While every care has been taken to ensure correctness of information, it is obviously not possible to guarantee complete freedom from errors or omissions or to accept liability arising from such errors or omissions. Therefore, any individual that uses the information contained within, or elects to perform or participate in do-it-yourself repairs or modifications acknowledges that there is a risk factor involved and that the publisher or its associates cannot be held responsible for personal injury or property damage resulting from the use of the information or the outcome of such procedures.

WARNING!

One final word of advice, this publication is intended to be used as a reference guide, and when in doubt the reader should consult with a qualified technician.

CONTENTS

CHAP.		PAGE
	PREFACE	
	LIST OF ILLUSTRATIONS	
I.	THE RALEIGH RANGE	1
II.	HOW THE ENGINE WORKS	13
III.	PRELIMINARIES	26
IV.	DRIVING	32
V.	ROADSIDE REPAIRS	44
VI.	OVERHAULING AND HINTS AND TIPS	56
VII.	SPEED WORK AND TRIAL RIDING	75
VIII.	TOURING	80
IX.	MOTOR CYCLING FOR LADIES (BY MISS MARJORIE COTTLE)	86
X.	LEGAL HINTS	91
XI.	SECOND-HAND MACHINES	97
XII.	USEFUL INFORMATION AND TABLES	101
	LIST OF RALEIGH SPARE PARTS STOCKISTS	105
	GLOSSARY OF MOTOR-CYCLING TERMS	116
	INDEX	131

ILLUSTRATIONS

FIG.		PAGE
1.	2·25 h.p. model, MG30	2
2.	2·98 h.p. model, MO30	3
3.	4·96 h.p. model, MA30	4
4.	3·48 h.p. 2-port sports model, MT30	5
5.	4·96 h.p. 2-port sports model, MH30	7
6.	4·96 h.p. combination, MA30	8
7.	4·96 h.p. combination, MH30	9
8.	Dual purpose combination, as pleasure vehicle	9
9.	Dual purpose combination, as delivery vehicle	10
10.	O.H.V. 2-port cylinder head	11
11.	The four-stroke engine	14
12.	The overhead valve Raleigh engine	16
13.	A sectional view of the Amal carburettor	17
14.	The Sturmey-Archer three-speed countershaft gear and parts used for the clutch	20
15.	Two of Mr. Mockford's wonderful jumping feats on his Raleigh	21
16.	The Raleigh controls	22
17.	The mechanism of the internal-expanding brake	23
18.	The Brooks super sports saddle	24
19.	The Raleigh twin pannier petrol tanks	34
20.	Traffic signals for use at corners	40
21.	How to remove the rear wheel	45
22.	The contact-breaker of the magneto	51
23.	Diagram showing how to adjust the tappets	53
24.	How to remove an O.H.V. push-rod	58
25.	Removing cylinder head of the O.H.V. engine	59
26.	A simple method of removing piston rings	60
27.	Diagram showing how too much valve grinding will wear away the valve seating	61
28.	View of the 3·48 h.p. super sports, showing timing gear and magneto chain cover removed	63
29.	The important parts of the machine requiring lubrication	66

ILLUSTRATIONS

FIG.		PAGE
30.	The 1930 front fork, showing nipples for use with the Enot's grease gun system and how to adjust the fork	68
31.	Showing thumb-screw adjustment for rear brakes	69
32.	Wiring diagrams for electric lamps	71
33.	How to align the sidecar	73
34.	Diagram illustrating reach of sparking plug	73
35.	Pistons used in Raleigh engines	75
36.	Diagram illustrating difference in wind resistance offered by upright and crouching riders	78
36A.	A Wayside Halt	82
37.	Specimen map from the Dunlop Guide	83
38.	Miss Marjorie Cottle and her 3·48 h.p. Raleigh semi-sports model	87
39.	Conventional road signs	95

THE RALEIGH HANDBOOK

CHAPTER I

THE RALEIGH RANGE

INTRODUCTION—Description of models—Types to choose.

THERE are five models marketed, ranging from 2·25 h.p. to 4·96 h.p., and although few in number there is a machine for almost every purpose. Most readers of this book will certainly have heard of the reliability of these machines, whether in trials or in everyday use. The Raleigh Company owes much to Mr. D. R. O'Donovan for his work in " hotting up " Raleigh engines, and 90 m.p.h. machines can now be bought at a very reasonable figure. These models make excellent mounts for those who go in for racing, whether on the road or track. It may be of interest to readers to know that the engines are manufactured by Sturmey-Archer, Ltd., as are the gear-boxes fitted to all Raleighs.

Numerous improvements have been made since the second edition of this book, the most notable being dry sump lubrication, which is employed on the 2·98 h.p. and larger models. This system will be fully described in a later chapter, but it may be as well to state here that simplicity, economy, and clean lines are among the many advantages secured by this type of lubrication. A specification is given below of the complete range of models, beginning with the 2·25 and working upwards in order of horse-power.

The 2·25 h.p. MG 30. This machine is introduced for the rider who requires a light, handy mount, coupled with reliability and economy.

ENGINE. 2·25 h.p. side valves, of Raleigh design and manufacture, the bore and stroke being 60 mm. × 79·5 mm., giving 225 c.c. capacity. Roller bearing big end, and ball bearing crankshaft. Aluminium piston with floating gudgeon pin.

LUBRICATION. Mechanical, with sight feed pump and reserve hand pump. Oil feed taken direct to crankshaft big end. Frame parts by grease gun.

IGNITION. B.T.-H. magneto with handlebar control. A large metal shield protects the magneto from dust or mud thrown up by the front wheel.

GEAR-BOX. Sturmey-Archer three-speed gear. Kick-starter. Handlebar controlled clutch. Gear ratios: 6·2, 9·6, and 17·2 to 1.

TRANSMISSION. Brampton chain, ½ in. × ·205 in. Chain case fully protecting front chain and top portion of rear one.

FIG. 1.—THE 2·25 H.P. MODEL

CONTROLS. Left hand: valve lifter, clutch, and magneto advance. Right hand: carburettor, front brake, and gear change lever.

FRONT FORKS. Of special design providing large movement. Fitted with single taper compression spring and spring-loaded shock absorbers.

HANDLEBAR. Adjustable, fitted with rubber grips.

TANKS. Special twin pannier tanks, concealing top tube, providing capacity for 1¼ gallons of petrol and 2 pints of oil.

SADDLE. Flexible top type. Saddle height (with rider seated), 24½ in.

FOOTRESTS. Adjustable, fitted with large rubber pads.

BRAKES. Internal expanding type fitted to front and rear

THE RALEIGH RANGE

wheels. Front operated by right-hand inverted lever. Rear operated by left toe pedal.

SILENCER. Bright chromium-plated silencer system with expansion chamber at rear.

CARRIER. Tubular, of sturdy construction.

STANDS. Front and rear of tubular construction.

TOOLBAG. Fitted to seat tube, complete with kit of tools and grease gun.

FIG. 2.—THE 2·98 H.P. MODEL

TYRES. Dunlop cord, 25 × 3·00 W.O. type.

MUDGUARDS. Plain section front and rear. Rear mudguard 5¼ in. wide.

LICENCE HOLDER. Mounted on front fork.

FINISH. Black enamel on coslet. Tank black cellulose with cream panel. Handlebar and bright parts chromium plated.

DIMENSIONS. Overall length, 82 in. Width, 30 in. Ground clearance, 4¾ in.

WEIGHT. 190 lb. less tools. TAX. 30s.

The 2·98 h.p. Model MO 30. This model is an example of the advance of modern design, employing as it does dry sump lubrication, enclosed tappets, and valve springs, etc.

ENGINE. 2·98 h.p. Raleigh design and manufacture, the bore

THE RALEIGH HANDBOOK

and stroke being 65·6 mm. × 88 mm. giving a total capacity of 298 c.c. Roller bearing big end. Ball bearing crankshaft. Aluminium piston with fully floating gudgeon pin.

LUBRICATION. Dry sump, entirely automatic. Oil feed taken direct to big end. Special provision made for lubricating timing gear. Operation of oil system may be verified by removing oil-filler cap. Frame parts by grease gun.

Except for the capacity of the tanks (1¾ gallons petrol and

FIG. 3.—THE 4·96 H.P. MODEL

2½ pints of oil) and the weight (208 lb.), the specification is as for the MG 30.

The 4·96 h.p. Model MA 30. An excellent machine for touring, either solo or with sidecar. This machine is of sturdy construction, and although not over fast, will be found to hold a very high average. A brief specification is given below.

ENGINE. 4·96 h.p., bore 79 mm., stroke 101 mm., 496 c.c. capacity. Internal flywheel, double row roller bearing big end. Aluminium piston, fitted with fully floating gudgeon pin. Crankshaft mounted on ball and roller bearings. Interchangeable valves.

LUBRICATION. Dry sump.

GEAR-BOX. Sturmey-Archer three-speed. Multi-plate clutch, handlebar controlled. Shock absorber incorporated in clutch. Kick-starter. Gear ratios: 5·2, 7·6, and 13·8 to 1.

TRANSMISSION. Brampton chain, lubricated by crankcase release. Front chain completely protected by chain case. Rear chain protected by chain cover.

FRONT FORKS. Sports type fitted with single taper compression spring and spring-loaded shock absorbers. Long bearings are provided at all moving points. A steering damper is incorporated, adjustable from above handlebar.

TANK. Petrol capacity is provided by twin tanks which con-

FIG. 4. THE 3·48 H.P. TWO-PORT SPORTS MODEL

ceal the top and tank tubes. Each tank is independent, and a total capacity of 2¾ gallons is provided. Oil is carried in a separate tank on down tube, which holds 3 pints.

TYRES. Dunlop cord, 26 × 3·25 W.O. type.

WEIGHT. 304 lb.

The 3·48 h.p. O.H.V. Two-Port Sports Model MT 30.

This is essentially a sportsman's machine, and is capable of very high speeds. Designed to give effortless, silent speed with economy and reliability.

ENGINE. 3·48, bore 71 mm., stroke 88 mm., 348 c.c. capacity. Roller bearing big end. Roller and ball bearing crankshaft. Aluminium piston fitted with fully floating gudgeon pin. Enclosed overhead rocker gear, push rod operated and provided with adequate provision for lubrication and dust exclusion.

LUBRICATION. Dry sump, entirely automatic.

IGNITION. B.T.-H. magneto with handlebar control.

GEAR-BOX. Sturmey-Archer three speed. Handlebar controlled clutch. Kick-starter. Gear ratios: 5·7, 7·6, and 13·7 to 1.

TRANSMISSION. Brampton chain, lubricated by crankcase release. Front chain completely protected by chain case. Rear chain protected by chain cover.

CONTROLS. Left hand: valve lifter, clutch, and magneto. Right hand: carburettor, front brake, and gear change lever.

FRONT FORKS. Sports type fitted with single taper compression spring and spring-loaded shock absorbers. Long bearings are provided at all moving points. A steering damper is incorporated, adjustable from above handlebar.

HANDLEBAR. Adjustable and underslung, fitted with rubber grips.

TANK. Petrol capacity is provided by twin tanks which conceal the top and tank tubes. Each tank is independent, and a total capacity of $2\frac{3}{4}$ gallons is provided. Oil is carried in a separate tank on down tube which holds 3 pints.

SADDLE. Flexible top type, giving riding position of 26 in. (with rider seated).

FOOTRESTS. Adjustable, giving three positions.

BRAKES. Internal expanding type fitted to front and rear wheels. Front operated by right-hand inverted lever. Rear operated by left toe pedal.

SILENCER. Bright chromium plated exhaust pipes to expansion chambers at rear.

STANDS. Front and rear, of tubular construction. Rear stand spring operated.

TOOLBAG. Fitted to seat tube, complete with kit of tools and grease gun.

TYRES. Dunlop cord, $26 \times 3 \cdot 25$ W.O. type.

MUDGUARDS. Front and rear guards of plain section.

LICENCE-HOLDER. Mounted on front fork.

FINISH. Black enamel on coslet. Tank finished in black cellulose with cream panel. Handlebar and usual parts chromium plated.

DIMENSIONS. Overall length, $86\frac{1}{2}$ in. Overall width, 32 in. Ground clearance, $4\frac{3}{8}$ in.

WEIGHT. 302 lb.

The 4·96 Two-Port Sports Model MH 30. This machine is practically identical with the MT 30 except for the following items: The bore and stroke of the engine are 79 mm. × 101 mm. respectively, giving a total capacity of 496 c.c. Gear ratios are 5·2, 6·9, and 12·4 to 1, and the weight is 322 lb.

Sidecar Models. The descriptions and specifications of the solo machines having come to an end, we will now take the combination models.

THE RALEIGH RANGE

The 4·96 h.p. Combination, Model MA 30. This consists of the 4·96 h.p. model as standard specification, but with touring handlebars and gear ratios of 5·8, 8·5, and 15·6 to 1. Touring sidecar complete with windscreen and coverall apron. Body, coach finish, upholstered in black and red, and fitted with locker at rear.

The 4·96 h.p. Combination, Model MH 30. This sporting outfit consists of the 4·96 O.H.V. and the sports sidecar, which has a

Fig. 5.—The 4·96 h.p. Two-Port Sports Model

roomy body and is comfortably upholstered in red, and fitted with locker at rear. Complete with screen and apron. The chassis is finished in black enamel, while the body is in frosted aluminium.

Other Sidecars. The Raleigh Co. also manufacture several other sidecars, among which are the Super Sports, Launch, and Lightweight models.

The Dual Purpose Combination. This sidecar is specially designed for use in conjunction with the 4·96 h.p. model, the combination combining all the advantages of the MA 30 with the utility of the tradesman's carrier. The lower portion of the body follows the lines of the sidecar fitted to the MA 30, and it is claimed that no difference can be detected when in use for passenger carrying. The seat, back upholstery, and arm rests are removable, when the top can be placed in position and secured by means of four turn-buckles. The change-over can be effected in a matter of three minutes only. The back panel is hinged and opens downwards to give access to lower portion of the body.

Fig. 6.—The 4·96 h.p. Combination Model

Trays can be supplied for the top portion at extra charge, also a child's seat for attachment in rear of body.

Buying a Machine. Raleigh dealers are dotted all over the country, in every town of any pretensions and in most large villages; but if the would-be rider is in doubt as to the location of the nearest dealer, he should write to the Raleigh Co., who will be pleased to supply him with the name and address on receipt of a post card.

Most of the dealers, and certainly the larger ones, stock a fairly comprehensive selection of Raleighs (a list of the spare parts stockists is given on pp. 105–114); and the best line to follow if you are contemplating purchasing a machine is to go and see your local dealer and inspect his stock, when he will be only too

Fig. 7.—The 4·96 h.p. Combination Model

Fig. 8.—Dual Purpose Combination, as Pleasure Vehicle

pleased to give you the benefit of his advice and experience in choosing the machine and power suited to your needs.

Types of Machines. If the prospective purchaser wishes a machine on which he will want to " potter," whether for pleasure or business purposes, the 2·98 h.p. model is the machine to

FIG. 9.—DUAL PURPOSE COMBINATION, AS DELIVERY VEHICLE

use. Although it is capable of 45 miles per hour, it is flexible enough to be equally suitable for tedious traffic work.

However, if the buyer has a family, or other inducements which will tempt him to purchase a sidecar later on, then the 4·96 h.p. machine should be carefully examined, as this machine will comfortably take a sidecar later on, if need should arise.

On the other hand, should the purchaser have occasional or permanent cravings for speed, the 3·48 h.p. overhead valve sports model is the speed-de-luxe model of the range. This latter machine is capable of its 85 miles per hour, and the expert can tune it up to perform even greater deeds.

Engines. Before proceeding with Chapter II, a few words with regard to the Raleigh power units will not be amiss.

The new overhead valve cylinder head is illustrated in Fig. 10, and it will be seen that this is a fine piece of work. It has been very carefully designed, and is provided with ample finning to

THE RALEIGH RANGE

SUMMARY OF MODELS

Model	Price 1930		Tax p.a.		Weight	Horse-power	Gear Ratios
	£	s.	£	s.	lb.		
MG 30	36	–	1	10	190	2·25	6·2; 9·6; 17·2
MO 30	37	10	1	10	208	2·98	6·2; 9·6; 17·2
MA 30	45	10	3	–	304	4·96	5·2; 7·6; 13·8
MT 30	48	–	3	–	302	3·48	5·7; 7·6; 13·7
MH 30	49	–	3	–	322	4·96	5·2; 6·9; 12·2
MA 30 combination	62	–	4	–	391	4·96	5·8; 8·5; 15·6
MH 30 combination	65	10	4	–	420	4·96	5·8; 7·8; 14
Dual purpose combination	66	–	4	–	460	4·96	5·8; 8·5; 15·6

distribute heat evenly, thus ensuring maximum efficiency under all conditions. The rockers are semi-enclosed with a consequent

FIG. 10. THE RE-DESIGNED RALEIGH TWIN-PORT CYLINDER HEAD USED ON THE 3·48 H.P. AND 4·96 H.P. O.H.V. MODELS

reduction in wear and less noise. Special attention has been paid to the timing gear in this respect, and noise has now been practically eliminated. Referring to Fig. 10, it will be seen that powerful concentric coil rocker return springs are employed. These keep the ends of the rocker arms clear of the valve stems when the valves are closed and the push rods fully depressed, thus at all times maintaining proper contact between the push rods and the rockers, and permitting the valve clearance to be accurately checked. The top cap of the rocker box is detachable after removing two screws, and adjustment of the tappets is effected after raising the telescopic tubes enclosing the push rods.

CHAPTER II

HOW THE ENGINE WORKS

THE principle of the motor-cycle engine—Engine—Carburettor—Magneto—Gear-box—Drive—Features of Raleigh design and reasons for their adoption.

IT is well known that the energy which propels the motor-cycle and its owner is derived from the explosive energy of petrol gas.

Broadly speaking, a motor-cycle power unit consists of three main parts : firstly, the engine itself ; the carburettor, which turns the petrol into an inflammable gas ; and the magneto, which supplies a spark at the correct moment to ignite the gas, explode it, and cause the engine to perform its allotted task.

Types of Engines. There are two broad classes into which all engines—whether motor-cycle or car engines—can be divided, namely, the two-stroke and the four-stroke engine.

Fig. 11 is a diagram of a four-stroke single-cylinder engine (such as the 2·98 h.p. and 4.96 h.p. Raleigh engines). Two parts of the engine in this diagram are heavily outlined ; the outer part is termed the cylinder ; and the inner part, which moves up and down in it, is termed the piston. If a cocoa tin were placed in a slightly larger tin, so that it could move up and down freely in it, it would exactly represent the cylinder and piston of our motor-cycle engine.

The reader need not concern himself with the two-stroke engine or the principles on which it works. He need only know that the difference between a two-stroke and a four-stroke engine lies in the fact that in the former there is a *power* stroke every second stroke ; in the latter there is a power stroke every fourth stroke.

All the Raleigh engines are of the latter type, because for all-round service a four-stroke engine is more durable and reliable than a two-stroke, especially for powers about 2½ h.p.

To turn back again to Fig. 11, and using this in conjunction with the following explanation of the theory of a four-stroke engine's working, the various functions of the four strokes of the piston will be easily seen.

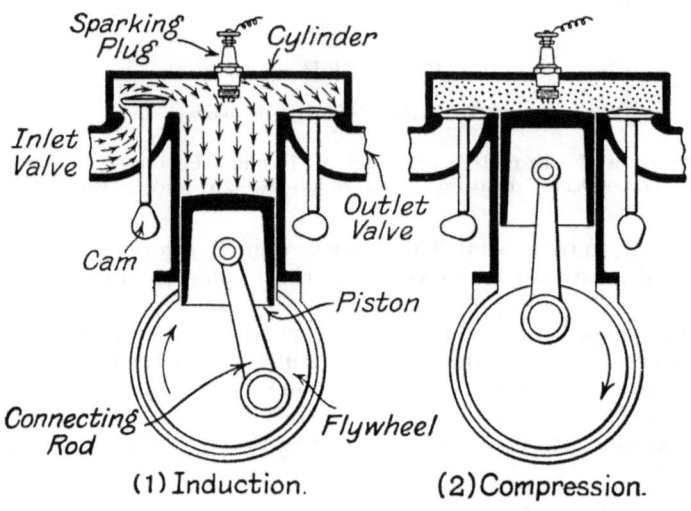
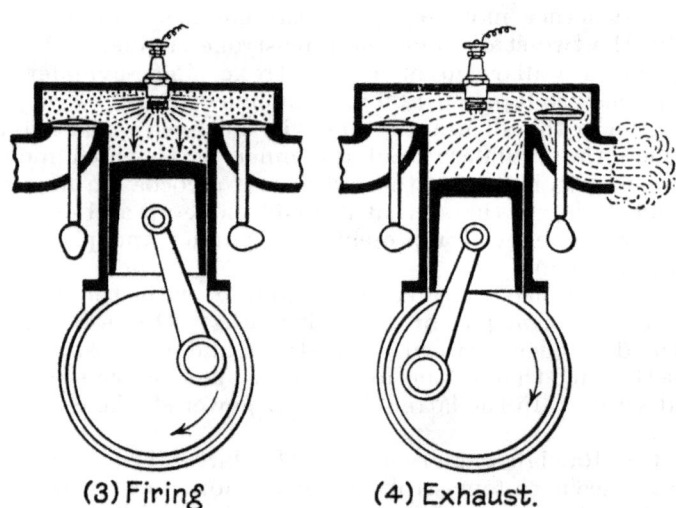

Fig. 11.—THE FOUR-STROKE ENGINE

Note the positions of the piston and valves during each of the four strokes

HOW THE ENGINE WORKS

Gas, when exploded, expands rapidly; therefore the object aimed at in designing a motor-cycle engine is to introduce a charge of gas into the cylinder at the correct moment, ignite the charge when the piston is at the top of the cylinder, so that the exploding gas will force the piston down the cylinder and thus turn the flywheel.

Supposing the piston is at the top of its stroke and is just commencing its downward stroke; in the illustration the inlet valve will be noticed to have been raised by a cam and to have opened the aperture which it has hitherto kept closed. On the opening of this valve, the suction exerted by the descending piston draws a charge of gas into the cylinder. Fig. 11 (1).

The piston, having reached the bottom of its stroke, then commences to travel upwards again. By this time the inlet cam has turned and has allowed the valve to close again, so that, with both valves closed, the charge of gas is tightly compressed in the cylinder. Fig. 11 (2).

As soon as the piston reaches the top of its stroke again, a spark occurs at the points of the sparking plug. This, of course, explodes the charge of gas, sending the piston down to the bottom of the cylinder with great force. Fig. 11 (3).

The momentum of the flywheel keeps the piston on the move and forces it up the cylinder again. By this time, the exhaust valve cam has opened its valve, so that the burnt gases can escape through into the exhaust pipe. Fig. 11 (4). The piston then commences its downward stroke again, the exhaust valve closes, and the inlet valve opens, and a fresh charge of gas is drawn into the cylinder, and the cycle repeated.

And so it goes on, inlet stroke, compression stroke, explosion stroke and exhaust stroke, each in turn, giving the name to this type of engine—the four-stroke engine.

Fig. 12 shows a cut-away view of the Raleigh overhead-valve engine, from which the same cycle of operations may be followed.

The Carburettor. As petrol is a liquid, some means must be found to turn it quickly into a gas, and to do this is the function of the carburettor. As everybody knows, petrol has a smell and is readily inflammable, for it fairly quickly turns into a gas on exposure to the atmosphere. Therefore the original form of carburettor consisted of a chamber where the surface of the petrol was made as large as possible and the gas which was given off from the surface was taken straight into the cylinder.

For a modern high-speed engine this method would be far from satisfactory, as petrol vaporizes too slowly, and therefore another and more efficient system has had to be devised.

Fig. 12.—The Overhead-valve Raleigh Engine

HOW THE ENGINE WORKS

The principle of the Amal carburettor, which is the type of carburettor used on Raleigh engines, is shown in Fig. 13. In this is shown the float chamber containing the float which keeps the petrol at the correct level. When the petrol level falls, the

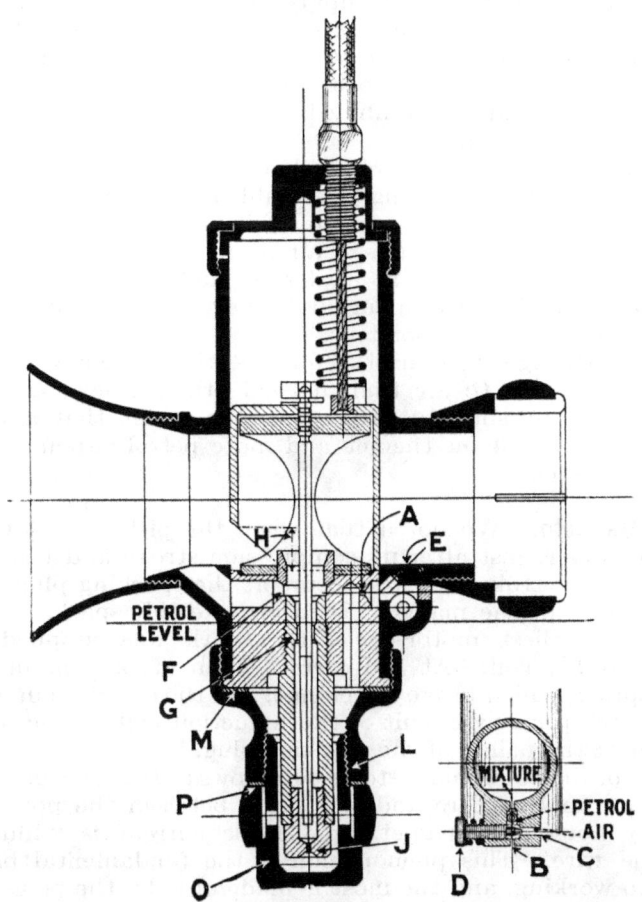

Fig. 13.—A Sectional View of the Amal Carburettor

float sinks, and with it the needle, allowing petrol to flow in through the petrol supply pipe, until the petrol level in the float chamber is sufficient to raise the float and the needle high enough to cut off the supply.

The petrol supply is arranged to be the same height as the jet or sprayer, or, if anything, slightly higher, so that when the petrol in the float chamber is at its correct level, petrol also reaches the top of the sprayer. The suction of the engine does the rest of the work. On the inlet stroke, it will be remembered that the descending piston exerts a suction. Therefore, if both air and petrol slides in the carburettor be open, this suction will draw in air through the air supply and also petrol through the jet. The sprayer has a number of finely-bored holes and, as the petrol is sucked out of it, it forms a fine spray, which, by the time it reaches the engine, becomes a gas. Air is drawn in at the same time, and the combined mixture of gas and air is thus drawn into the cylinder.

Petrol gas by itself cannot explode ; the addition of oxygen is needed, and air, possessing the double advantage of containing oxygen and being cheap, is used for this purpose. Theoretically, between five and seven parts of air to one part of petrol gas are needed to cause an efficient explosion, and the sizes of the air inlet ports and the jet of a carburettor are so arranged that they will give the correct proportions.

When a stronger mixture is required—that is to say, a greater proportion of gas to air than normal—the air lever is closed, allowing the air slide to drop, with the result that a greater suction is imposed on the jet and more petrol vapour is taken into the engine.

The Magneto. We noted that when the piston is at the top of the cylinder, just after its compression stroke and just before the explosion stroke, a spark occurs at the sparking plug points. The function of the magneto is to provide this spark.

On the earliest motor-cycles the spark was supplied by a battery and a coil. At the correct moment, a cam moved a metal spring, which broke the circuit, and the cessation of current through the primary circuit of the induction coil caused a spark to occur at the points of the sparking plug.

The working of a magneto is as follows: If a coil of wire be wound on an iron core and is rotated between the poles of an ordinary horseshoe magnet, an electric current is " induced " into the wire. This phenomenon is the fundamental basis of magneto working, and the most is made of it by the poles of the magnet being shaped in segments of a circle and the rotating core, termed the " armature," being wound closely. The turning of the armature between the poles of the magnet generates a weak current in this coil of wire, which is known as the primary coil of the magneto to distinguish it from the secondary coil, which will be mentioned later. Then a mechanically-operated contact breaker makes and breaks the current in the primary circuit at the required moments. Then, in the same manner as in an induction coil, the breaking of the primary circuit causes a

HOW THE ENGINE WORKS

corresponding current of greater voltage in the secondary coil, which is a coil of very fine and long wire wound round outside the primary coil. This secondary current, which is at a very much higher tension or voltage than the primary current, is led to the sparking plug, causing a spark to jump across its points, igniting the compressed charge of gas in the cylinder.

Thus at every revolution of the magneto armature one spark is delivered across the points of the sparking plug, but in a four-stroke engine one spark is required only at every fourth stroke or two complete revolutions of the flywheel. Therefore the magneto has to be run at exactly half the speed of the engine, so that it will deliver a spark every other revolution of the engine as required.

In the case of a twin-cylinder engine the magneto is required to supply a spark to *each cylinder* every two revolutions, i.e. one spark per revolution. The connection is made between the magneto and each plug in turn by a special device termed a distributor. A full discussion of the theory and construction of the magneto would occupy too much space in this book. Readers desiring further information are referred to the special books on this subject.

Valve-timing Mechanism. As shown in Fig. 11, the valves are opened by means of cams, the valves being closed by means of their springs. A study of the diagram will show that the valve cams also have to perform only one revolution while the flywheel performs two. To do this, the valve cams therefore have to be run, like the magneto, at half-engine speed.

In Fig. 11 the valves are shown as opened by two separate cams, for the sake of clearness ; but in the Raleigh engine both the valves are operated by a single cam. The pinion revolves, at half engine speed, in anti-clockwise direction, opening the exhaust valve and inlet valve in turn.

In actual practice, the cam does not push the valve direct, or undue friction and side pressure would be set up. Therefore, in the Raleigh engine, the cam operates rockers which, in their turn, push up their respective valve tappets with a minimum of friction.

In all models the timing pinion teeth are marked with punch holes to indicate the teeth which are to engage, thus rendering reassembling as near " fool-proof " as humanly possible.

Gear-box. All Raleigh motor-cycles are fitted with the Sturmey-Archer three-speed countershaft gear, as illustrated in Fig. 14. This illustrates the type of gear as fitted to the 3·48 h.p. and 4·96 h.p. models.

The outstanding feature of this gear-box is that the three speeds and the kick-starter are provided by means of only three pairs of pinions, which are constantly in mesh. Any chance or possibility of stripping the gears through faulty changing is thereby avoided. The kick-starter mechanism is entirely enclosed.

The Sturmey-Archer gear compensator is now included inside the gear-box, instead of being, as formerly, incorporated with the change-speed lever. This compensator consists of a strong spring enclosed in a cylinder and incorporated with the lever

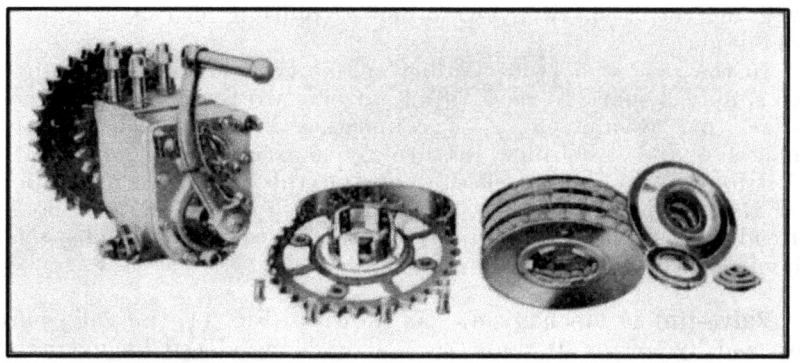

Fig. 14.—The Sturmey-Archer Three-speed Countershaft Gear and Parts used for the Clutch

moving the two free pinions and dogs. Should the dogs not be in the correct position to engage immediately the change-speed lever is moved, the spring allows the lever to be moved into position and then sustains a pressure on the dogs until they are in their correct positions.

The Shock Absorber. On all-chain models, some form of shock absorber is necessary, and this is incorporated in the clutch sprocket. A series of rubber buffers, taking up very little space and light in weight, remove any unevenness of drive at low speeds.

Lubrication. The question of lubrication is an important one as far as a motor-cycle is concerned, and a new feature is the adoption of dry sump lubrication on the 2·98 h.p. and larger models. On the 2·25 h.p. the oiling is by a mechanical sight feed pump, and this will be described first.

The plunger itself is rotated by means of a worm, which is

FIG. 15.—Two of Mr. Mockford's Wonderful Jumping Feats on his Raleigh

integral with the driving dog. The projection on the right-hand end of the plunger bears against a face cam, thus imparting a reciprocating movement. The two ports, one at either end of the plunger, are timed to operate at the correct moment, passing along a supply of oil in drops through the union which connects the oil pipe to the engine, and is proportionate to the engine's speed.

The setting of the regulator is a matter for the rider's own

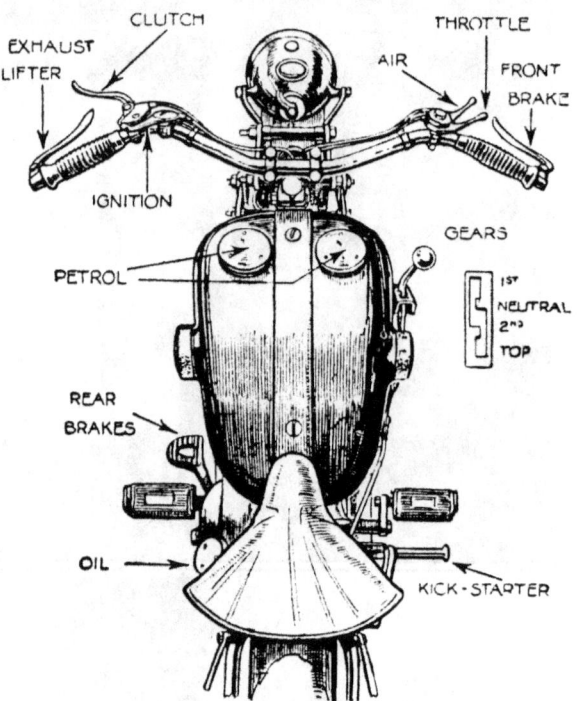

From the Motor Cycle.
FIG. 16.—THE RALEIGH CONTROLS

judgment and should vary according to the speed of the machine and the different grades of oil used under different temperatures.

The Dry Sump System. The oil is distributed by means of a reciprocating plunger pump of generous dimensions, driven by spur gear and worm from the crankshaft pinion. Oil is collected by the pump from the top oil union, and is passed through the centre of the driving worm shaft into the timing cover bush. From here it is fed by internal ducts to the crankshaft, where the oil is taken direct to the big end. Oil is then fed by splash

HOW THE ENGINE WORKS

on to the cylinder walls, from whence it drains back to the crankcase and sump. A certain amount of oil is by-passed from the crankshaft feed direct into the timing box. This is picked up by the timing gears, and eventually collected in the bottom of the timing box and returned to the sump.

A filter of considerable area is provided in the sump, from the end of which the oil is collected by means of a copper tube, cast integral with the crankcase, and conveyed to the return side of the oil pump. Oil is returned to tank via the lower union. The

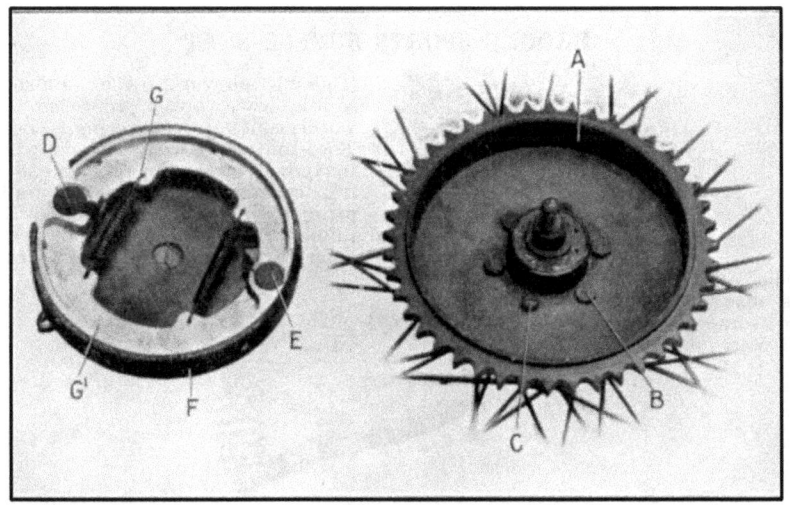

Fig. 17.—The Mechanism of the Internal-expanding Brake

crankcase breather is arranged on the driving side of engine, and provides lubrication for the front chain.

Providing there is an adequate supply of oil in the tank, oil will be fed to the mechanical pump, which will automatically supply the engine and return surplus to the tank.

Brakes. Brakes play a part of no little importance on a motor-cycle, for it is equally important for a machine to have efficient brakes as an efficient engine.

The brakes are of the external-expanding type, operating on large drums, delightfully easy and firm in action. As shown in Fig. 17, the brake consists of a drum A, on the inside of which are two semi-circular segments G^1, faced with Ferodo brake lining F. Pressure on the brake pedal causes the cam D to rotate, a partial turn thus pressing the two segments against the inside of the brake drum. When no pressure is exerted on the brake pedal, the two segments are held apart from the brake drum by the spring G, so that no friction takes place when the brake is out of use.

Springing. Effective suspension and springing play an important part in the design of a motor-cycle, both from the view of comfort of the rider and saving of wear and tear to the machine.

BROOKS SPORTS SUPPLE-SEAT

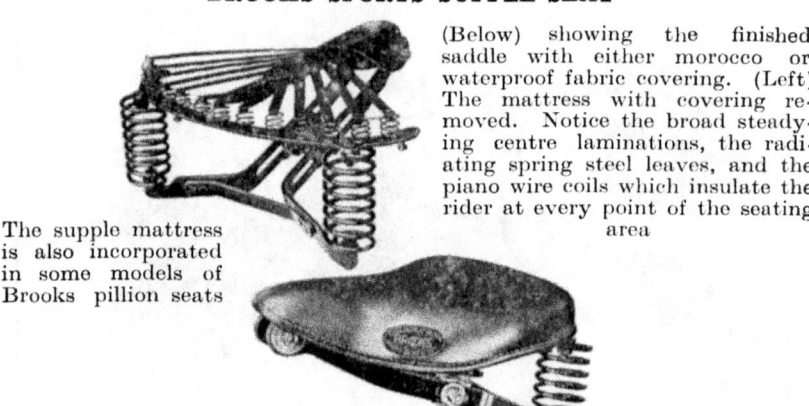

(Below) showing the finished saddle with either morocco or waterproof fabric covering. (Left) The mattress with covering removed. Notice the broad steadying centre laminations, the radiating spring steel leaves, and the piano wire coils which insulate the rider at every point of the seating area

The supple mattress is also incorporated in some models of Brooks pillion seats

FIG. 18.—THE BROOKS SPORTS SUPPLE-SEAT SADDLE

Were no spring forks used on a motor-cycle, it would be necessary for the frame to be of much stouter tubing to withstand the violent shocks. The handlebar would vibrate and would become too uncomfortable to hold.

Generally speaking, road shocks, in the form of bumps and pot-holes, tend to force the front wheel up in a line parallel with the steering head. To meet this requirement, it will be noted that the fork possesses a hinged movement, the amount of movement being controlled by a spring.

Saddles. Terry's or Brooks' saddle may be obtained, and the illustration above shows the internal construction of the Brooks "Supple-seat" saddle, and the method of springing each part of the saddle separately, ensuring the maximum of comfort on long rides.

HOW THE ENGINE WORKS 25

An interesting feature of the Brooks supple-seat is the patent damper pivot which enables the rider to control the degree of resiliency to suit riding conditions, i.e. tightened for speed work or slackened off for roadwork. Different riding weights can also be accommodated in a similar manner.

Knee Grips. These are fitted as standard to all models and greatly assist the rider to hold on to his machine when travelling over bad and indifferent road surfaces.

The Silencer. The law compels all motor-cycle engines to be fitted with silencers which will render them reasonably silent. If the exhaust gases were allowed their exit straight into the air, the noise of the explosions would be deafening and annoying. The efficiency of the design of an exhaust pipe and silencer is a most important item in motor-cycle construction, for if these are too small and of inefficient design, undue " back-pressure" is set up, which tends to overheat the engine and thus lessen its efficiency.

On the sports models, the exhaust pipe and silencer are of the " one piece " type, as a glance at the illustrations of the various models in Chapter I will show. In this silencer and exhaust pipe, and in that fitted to the O.H.V. models, absence of sharp bends and the large diameter of the exhaust pipes enable the exhaust gases to escape more quickly than they would otherwise be able to do.

Now that the Home Office is rather concerned over the noise which a minority of selfish motor-cyclists cause, it behoves us all to wend our ways as silently as possible. Raleigh riders need have few qualms that they will be summoned and prosecuted, because silence is a matter to which Raleigh designers have given great attention. In last year's London-Edinburgh run, for instance, the Raleigh was awarded the special prize for silence, while the manufacturers of the " Ghost " silencer, fitted to the 3·48 O.H.V. sports model (Fig. 4.) guarantee to indemnify the rider against fines, provided he does not tinker with the silencer, of course, and convert it to the stove-pipe type. So the Raleigh rider, at any rate on the score of noise, is well protected from police proceedings.

CHAPTER III

PRELIMINARIES

NECESSARY preliminaries—Hire purchase—Registration, taxes, number plates, driving licence, lamps, horn—Advisable preliminaries: Insurance, joining a club.

THIS chapter concerns more the prospective rider than the actual one. It is indeed primarily intended for the benefit of the man (or lady) who has recently chosen his or her machine. It will, however, be found to be of assistance also to those who have driven the same motor-cycle for years.

The majority of agents keep in stock a selection of machines suitable for all types of riders and their needs; but if the particular machine the prospective rider has in view is not in stock, the agent can normally obtain it in a few days from the Raleigh works (at Nottingham); or the rider may, if he wishes, go direct to the works to take delivery of his mount, the financial part of the business, whether paid outright or by instalments, making no difference whether delivery is taken at the works or at your local dealer's.

Hire Purchase. The Raleigh hire purchase system is simple and confidential. The company handles it all itself, without the usual intervention of some financial house, which takes no interest in you beyond getting your money and a very considerable sum in interest. Every Raleigh sold under their hire purchase system is insured for one year (for mutual protection), the cost of the insurance being included in and spread over the year's payments.

If the rider is an entire novice, or even has not had much experience of motor-cycling, it is far the better way to take delivery of the new machine from his local dealer. The already expert rider can, of course, go to the works and ride straight away.

NECESSARY PRELIMINARIES

Whichever course is pursued, there are a few preliminaries which have to be gone through before a motor-cycle may be taken and ridden on the road. In order that these items may be dealt with and completed before delivery of the machine is taken, the dealer should be asked to find out the following particulars, which will be required when the application form for a licence is filled in.

PRELIMINARIES

Registration. An application form for a licence for the motor-cycle can be obtained of any head Post Office, and has to be filled in as follows—

Description	" Motor-cycle."
If used for drawing trailer or sidecar	" Sidecar " or " No " to be filled in.
Name.	" Raleigh."
Type or model	Either the model No. from the catalogue may be filled in here, or the description " Semi-Sports Solo," " Touring Combination," etc.
H.P..	" 2·25," " 3·48," or " 4·96," as the case may be.
Engine No..	The local dealer or works can give this No. in advance of delivery.
Frame No..	do. do.
Weight	This can be arrived at from table on page 11, adding the weight of lamps, generator, and horn, which may be from 3 to 12 lb.
Number of wheels . . .	" Two." (The sidecar wheel is not considered.)
Annual rate of licence fee payable .	This can also be seen from the table on page 11.

The usual address where the machine is to be kept must also be filled in, and the applicant's full name and address.

The application form should then be posted off to the Licences Department of the County Council in whose area the machine is usually kept, and in most instances the licence will be sent back by return of post.

Annual renewals for this licence may be obtained on application at any head Post Office between the 1st and 15th of January each year. A Post Office can only issue renewals of the same type as that already held, that is to say, that an annual licence can only be renewed as an annual licence and a quarterly one as a quarterly one. If one wishes to change from annual to quarterly, or vice versa, application must be made to the County Council. Part term licences can now be obtained.

It should be remembered that the weight of the machine is the *unladen* weight, that is, minus tools, tool-bag, petrol, oil and accessories. For this purpose, the figures given in the table on page 11 may usually be taken as correct, with the addition of the weight of lamps, generator and horn.

Number Plates. The next legal necessity before a machine is ridden on the road is number plates. On the new licence the registration number of the machine will be given, and this number has to be painted on the two number plates in white letters on a black ground, conforming to the following dimensions—

Each figure or letter must be 1¾ in. deep by 1¼ in. wide, and $\frac{5}{16}$th of an inch thick at all parts. Between the top and bottom of the letters and the edge of the plate there must be a margin of at least ¼ of an inch and a margin of at least ½ in. at each side.

The letters must not be allowed to become obscured by mud or dust and the plates must not be covered in any way—a point to bear in mind when a pillion passenger is carried.

It may seem, on the surface, a very trivial item to insist on the numbers being of such exact dimensions, but this is a point the owner should bear well in mind, as the police in a few districts are strict on the observance of this regulation.

In the Road Vehicle Amendment Regulations it is proposed, as from 6th October, 1930, to increase the linear dimensions of the new rear number plate to approximately two-thirds those of the ordinary car plate, instead of one-half as at present.

Driving Licence. A driving licence is necessary before a machine may be ridden on the public highway. This is obtained from the County Council for a fee of 5s. per annum. An application should be sent with the 5s. to the County Council or local Borough Council. Personal application may be made for this (as well as the registration licence), if the rider wishes, but much time and trouble is saved by postal application.

If the rider is over 16 years of age,* a licence may be obtained to drive a motor-cycle only ; if he is over 17 years, it may be obtained to drive a motor-cycle and motor-car without extra cost. Therefore, if over 17, it is always advisable to apply for it to drive a motor-car as well, even if no such luxury is in view at the moment. Even if the applicant is over 17, the licence is made out to allow him to drive a motor-cycle only, unless he mentions on his application form that he wishes it to entitle him to drive a motor-car as well.

This licence must be carried on the person at all times when driving. It must be produced when a request is made for it by a police officer. Incidentally, the police officer is allowed to examine only the face of the licence ; he is not allowed to examine the back for endorsements, although, so long as the rider has a clear conscience, there is no object in annoying the officer by pointing this out to him—unless one is a stickler for principles. But there the law remains—he may examine the front and not the back, the point being that the discovery of a backful of endorsements might be inclined to prejudice him.

Audible Warning of Approach. The law compels a motor-cycle to be possessed of means by which " audible warning of approach "

* At the time of going to press this has not yet become law, but there are reasons to believe that this will be so at an early date.

PRELIMINARIES

may be given. A horn is the normal means for complying with this rule, although legally anything which will make a noise will do, such as a bell, drum, bugle, or whistle. Usually the best type of horn to use is the ordinary bulb type, of good quality, which gives a deep penetrating note. Some riders prefer mechanical horns, but these are liable to derangement. Usually the most reliable type is the ordinary bulb horn, which is extremely simple in construction, dust in the reed being the only trouble which is usually encountered.

ADVISABLE PRELIMINARIES

Though not legally necessary, there are one or two preliminaries which are well advisable for the rider to undertake before he takes his machine out on the road. Whereas the legal preliminaries are more for the benefit of other road-users, the following advisable preliminaries benefit the rider himself primarily and, incidentally, other road-users.

Insurance. By far and away the most necessary of these is the question of insurance. The " All-in " insurance policy saves the rider a great deal of time and inconvenience, for it covers his machine against theft, injury to machine, etc., and, what is more important, third-party risks.

If the rider is fortunate enough to be financially well-off, it is a comfort to know that one can always be in a position to pay any claims that may arise from " third-party " risk. And if the rider is not well-off, it is certainly his duty to insure himself against these risks. Supposing—and accidents are as often as not caused by another rider's carelessness—an accident occurs, injuring another person, or maybe a child runs across the road and it is impossible to avoid running him down. The luckless rider, even if he escapes injury himself, may fatally or seriously injure the " third-party " ; a court may subsequently award high damages to this third-party ; and if the rider is not in a position to pay this compensation, he runs the risk of being seriously embarrassed, financially, for years.

And, whether the accident to the third party be the rider's own fault or not, it is certainly his moral duty to insure himself against third-party risks, for it is unfair that a citizen should be liable to be injured by traffic and yet be unable to obtain compensation.

It should be remembered, when taking out a policy, that premiums will probably be less if the owner rides the machine himself and allows no one else to do so, as an extra premium is charged if the rider wishes another rider of the same machine to be covered as well. Also, rebates may be obtained from most companies if the machine is used for private purposes only, if the rider agrees to pay, say, 10 per cent of every claim himself (this should exclude " third-party " risks) ; and, later on, if no claim is made on the company for two years, or the value of the machine reduced, a further reduction in the premium may be obtained. Careful consideration of the conditions for obtaining rebates is well worth while.

Within the last few years premiums on motor-cycles have soared somewhat, but it seems now that the limit has been reached, and it is to be hoped that within a year or two premiums will again sink to a level more suited to the average rider's pocket.

Joining a Club. There are few districts now which are not possessed of a motor-cycling club, and there are several advantages to be gained from joining one. For solo riders especially, much useful information may be gained from fellow-members ; and as the majority of them have practical experience, the information gleaned is usually worth its weight in gold to a novice.

The novice need have no fear of joining a local club, just because he is a novice. The writer personally is in touch with many clubs, and does not know of one which does not genuinely welcome new members. If a club is to live, it must obtain a good supply of new members each year, and so the rider need not be afraid that he will be the only tyro there ! There are also some " Raleigh " clubs, whose members are all Raleigh riders.

Apart from this, a motor-cycling club forms a very convenient meeting-place for young people who have the same inclinations and hobbies. Every young man of to-day knows how difficult it is to get hold of others to mix with ; but this difficulty can soon be got over by joining a club, with its club runs, outings, and social events, which all help to make the world go round a little more smoothly.

Many of these local clubs are affiliated to the Royal Automobile Club, and membership of the local club entitles him to many of the advantages of joining the R.A.C. direct. But it is also extremely useful to join one of the general road organizations as well as, or instead of, a local club.

These " road organizations " give the rider free legal defence ; a " get-you-home " scheme ; services of road guides and local representatives ; will map out your holiday tour free of charge, or give you advice as to road conditions ; will give you technical assistance ; supply you with lists of reliable hotels, in fact, approach the millennium as far as possible, and all for a merely nominal subscription of about a guinea a year.

PRELIMINARIES

The names and addresses of these organizations are given below, and details of subscriptions and advantages of membership will be gladly supplied by their respective secretaries—

The Raleigh Motor-Cycle Club, Nottingham.
Hon. Sec : B. F. C. Fellowes, 62 Warren Ave., Haydn Rd., Nottingham.
The Royal Automobile Club, 89–91 Pall Mall, London, S.W.1.
The Automobile Association, Fanum House, Whitcomb Street, W.C.2.
The Auto-Cycle Union, 83 Pall Mall, London, S.W.1.

The membership of the Raleigh Motor-cycle Club is by no means confined to Nottingham area, and the club has members in all parts of the country. They have a fine list of trophies for annual competition, including the President's Trophy, which is awarded annually for the best aggregate performance in the four principal reliability trials held during the year. It is well worth while writing to the secretary for particulars of membership of this club, which welcomes novices just as heartily as old Raleigh riders.

Of course, if the prospective rider intends to go in for competition work, membership of the particular club which runs the competition is essential. All the bigger motor-cycling competitions of the year are organized by the A.C.U., and to enter for these membership is essential. The A.A. and R.A.C. confine themselves more to road service, leaving the competition side of the pastime to the A.C.U. Therefore, for the budding competition star, the A.C.U. is of more service.

CHAPTER IV

DRIVING

PREPARATIONS for a run—The controls of the Raleigh—Starting the engine—The first spin—Tyres—Solo riding—Driving a combination—Hill work—Rules of the road—Driving in traffic—Night riding—Pillion riding.

As mentioned in the previous chapter, the engine and frame numbers of a new machine may generally be obtained from the local agent in advance ; and other necessary details, such as weight, obtained from the agent or the catalogue, so that the rider has been able to send in his application form for driving licence and registration licence before he takes over delivery of the new machine.

PREPARATIONS FOR A RUN

We will assume, therefore, that the reader has taken possession of his new machine and the eagerly-awaited day when the first run is to be taken has arrived. The licence is fixed on, the numbers are painted on the plates, the driving licence is in its place, the horn is fitted, and everything in legal order to take the machine on the road.

In the tool-bag of the machine will be found an envelope containing literature regarding the machine, and on the outside of the envelope will be found a list of the tools that the tool-bag should contain—if it is a new machine, of course. These should be carefully checked over and, if found wanting, complaint should be made to the local agent at once and the missing articles secured. The literature supplied with the machine is worth perusing, as it gives many useful hints and tips and aids in getting the best out of the machine.

First of all, place the machine on the stand by releasing the latter from its clip by a sharp downward tap with the foot, placing the foot on it when it reaches the ground, and pulling the machine backwards and upwards by the carrier. Avoid doing this by the saddle, or in time a saddle spring may be broken. On the MA, MT, and MH the rear stand is of the spring-up type.

The petrol tanks should be filled with petrol and the oil tank filled with oil of well-known reputation and quality, some oils being particularly recommended by the makers as being most satisfactory for their engines. Other grades and makes of oil may be used, if the rider wishes, but for all general purposes these will be found most suitable. As nothing can ruin an engine more quickly than cheap oil, with its low flashpoint, it cannot be too much emphasized how important it is to obtain oil that is good in quality.

The gear-box on a new machine needs no attention, as it is sent out filled with half a pound of " Speedwell Crimsangere," a special lubricant prepared for the gear-box makers. This is sufficient to last 1,000 miles, when a further ¼ lb. should be added.

The Controls of the Raleigh. Fig. 16 shows the Raleigh handlebar controls, which are arranged as follows: On the right handlebar, the front brake is in the usual position under the grip ; the air and throttle levers are placed on top of the bar, the longer (and lower) lever being the throttle control, which controls the amount of petrol supplied to the engine by the carburettor. The upper lever, the air lever, likewise controls the supply of air. Both controls open inwards, that is to say, air and petrol are both shut off from the engine when the levers are moved outwards as far as possible.

Underneath the left handlebar is the exhaust lifter, which raises the exhaust valve as an aid to starting, as explained below. The lever over the handlebar is the magneto control, which advances or retards the spark at will. A movement outwards retards the spark. The remaining lever on the left handlebar is the clutch control lever, which is situated below the left handlebar in a similar position to the exhaust valve lifter.

The special functions of the various levers are described below in the driving instructions for a first spin. By far the best system for the would-be rider to adopt in learning the handling of his motor-cycle is to get an expert friend to teach him the controls, their functions, and the method and time for using them. However, as it is essential, or at any rate wise, to acquire theoretical knowledge as well as a practical training, a study of the following paragraphs will be helpful before taking the machine out on the road for the first time.

To the present, the machine has been placed on the stand, the petrol and oil tanks have been filled, and the machine is ready to start off. Needless to say, it is only a solo machine which need be put up on the stand for this operation.

On machines fitted with the sight feed system of lubrication the hand pump should be used to give five charges of oil, and then the regulator should set almost fully open. After a few minutes' running the engine will commence to smoke from the exhaust pipe. Shut down the regulator a notch or two at a time, running the engine a few minutes after each alteration until only a faint blue smoke is apparent.

So far as the dry sump lubricated engines are concerned, however, it is only necessary to observe whether the oil is actually being returned to the tank, which may be verified by removal of the oil tank filler cap, when the flow of oil through the return pipe will be visible.

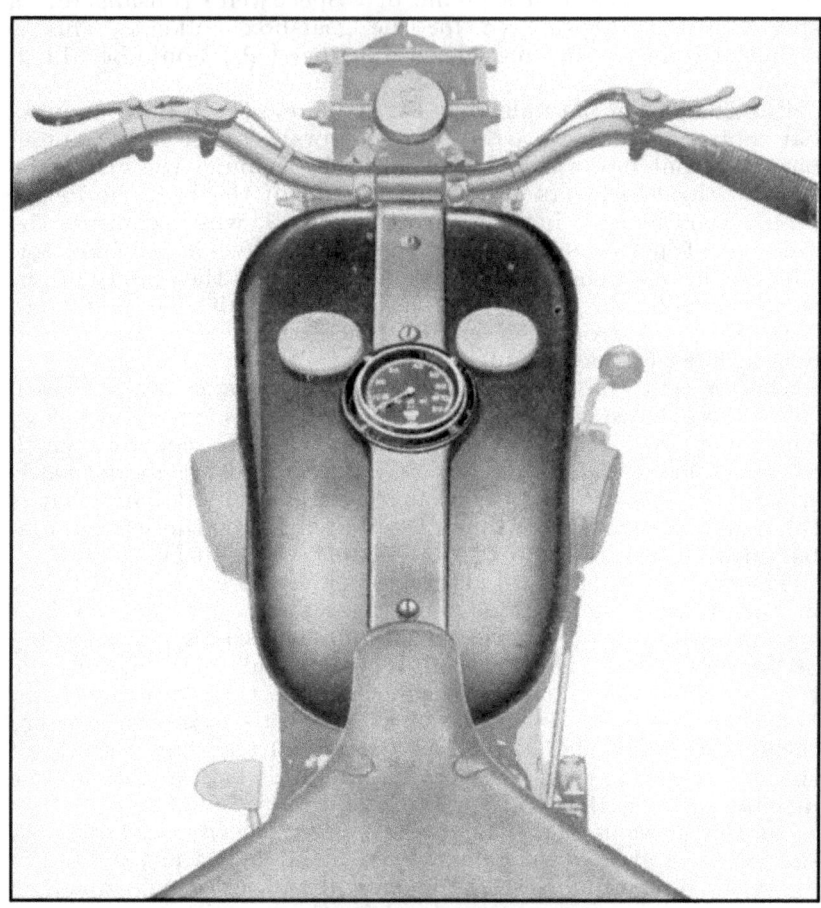

Fig. 19.—The Raleigh Twin Pannier Petrol Tanks

The next operation is to turn on the petrol.

First of all, flood the carburettor by depressing the needle momentarily, say, for 1 sec.; this is sufficient to flood the petrol above the level of the jet, for there is no need to wait until the petrol is actually dripping from underneath the jet.

DRIVING

Next, the throttle lever (right handlebar, bottom lever) should be opened about one-third of its total movement and the air lever one-quarter open. In some settings of carburettor it will be found that starting is easier when the air lever is left closed; but, generally speaking, it is better to have it slightly open. The magneto control lever (left handlebar) should be slightly retarded by being moved about a third of its movement outwards.

The kick-starter should then be pressed down until resistance is felt (caused by the compression of the engine). Then the kick-starter should be allowed to come to the top of the stroke again. The exhaust lever should be momentarily raised (to allow the engine to be turned over compression) and the kick-starter should be kicked down as sharply as possible. Two or three repetitions of this should start the engine.

The whole essence of the art of starting by kick-starter is to remember that it must be kicked *sharply*. A certain nervousness is always encountered when using a kick-starter for the first time, but this should be severely overcome. Occasionally the engine will fire before the piston has reached the top of its stroke, causing the engine to rotate in the wrong direction and thus forcing the kick-starter upwards—a little unnerving to the beginner, but nothing serious.

The machine started, the rider can then discover more easily the various functions of the controls. The air lever should be opened as far as possible, and the petrol lever closed as far as this can be done without stopping the engine. On no account should the engine be allowed to " race " when it is on the stand or in neutral gear, especially if it is a new engine. The magneto control should be advanced and retarded, the difference in the running speed of the engine being noted. The exhaust lifter may be raised and dropped again just in time to prevent the engine stopping.

Riding. Presuming that the engine has not been stopped by these experiments, after it has been ascertained that the gear lever is in the neutral position, the machine should be lowered from its stand, the latter being secured in its clip by a sharp upward movement.

Presuming that the rider has had previous bicycle experience and has mastered the art of balancing, it is safe for him to attempt to drive straight away; but if he is in doubt as to whether balancing can be accomplished safely, it is better to acquire this art by coasting the machine in neutral (without the engine running) down a slight incline. A few minutes of this will show the rider the ease with which a motor-cycle may be balanced, the weight of the machine almost making it balance itself.

To start the machine—with the engine running slowly raise the clutch lever and, keeping it raised, move the gear lever into the low gear position. Next, open the throttle slightly to accelerate the engine and at the same time gently lower the clutch lever. The clutch will then take up the drive and the machine will move forward. When sufficient speed has been attained, the rider may place his feet on the footrests and, if he feels that he has ample confidence, the clutch lever should again be raised and the gear lever moved into the next gear notch (that is to say, into the notch beyond the neutral notch), and the clutch lever lowered again gently. When a moderate speed has again been attained, the clutch may again be lifted and the gear lever moved right forward into top gear notch. When once top gear is attained, speed may be regulated by the throttle lever, accelerating slowly and evenly, as sudden acceleration and decelerations are bad for the tyres and transmission, and may cause side-slip.

As the rider becomes familiar with the controls, he will find that he is able to control the speed of his engine when changing gear more efficiently. When the clutch is out (lever raised), the engine should be throttled down so that it does not roar wildly during gear-changing operations. This, however, is an art acquired by experience only, and it will probably be a matter of a week or so before the rider can feel that he is sure of a quiet gear change. The gear lever should always be moved sharply into position. There is no fear of damaging the gear : firstly, because the gear wheels are in constant mesh, so that it is impossible to damage them, the changing being accomplished by sturdy " dog clutches," which are capable of withstanding any reasonable strain to which they are likely to be put ; and, secondly, because a compensating spring is incorporated in the gear-box, which, if the dogs are not opposite each other and ready to engage, keeps pressure on them until they are in such a position as to mesh with each other. There is thus no need for the rider to " feel " his gear, as in car practice.

Driving Hints. Air being cheaper than petrol, it is economical to run with the air lever as far open as possible, which will usually be found to be slightly more than half-way open. For slow riding, the air lever should be closed so as to be in about the same position as the petrol lever, the magneto control lever being retarded slightly at the same time.

For speeds above 15 miles per hour, on the level, the magneto control may, generally speaking, be fully advanced. On reaching a hill, or at any other time when the engine has to labour at all, it should be retarded.

Knocking. The curious sound known as "knocking" occurs in an engine when it is temporarily overloaded, such as on hill-climbing work. Knocking is a decided strain on the engine, and immediately it occurs, steps should be taken to prevent it by slightly closing the air lever; if this is ineffective, the ignition lever should be slightly retarded. If these two movements fail to stop the knock, the machine should be put into a lower gear.

Hill-climbing. One often hears riders boastfully telling tales of steep hills in the district which they claim to have climbed on top gear. While this may to a certain extent be a meritorious performance in an official trial, it is certainly a foolish practice for the general rider. To make a machine struggle up a steep hill on top gear, knocking wildly and heavily labouring, is bad for the engine and invariably denotes a bad rider. The gear-box is provided for use and the novice need not feel it is a disgrace to drop into second gear immediately the engine begins to labour. In this way he will lengthen the life of his engine immeasurably and, incidentally, climb the hill more quickly. The power of an engine depends on the number as well as the power of the explosions in its cylinder. This power increases with its speed in a far greater proportion than the actual speed ratio, up to a certain speed. Therefore dropping into second gear will usually increase the speed of the machine, owing to the greater power put out by the engine. When descending a steep hill, use the brakes alternately, if possible, to prevent excessive heat on rear brake.

Brakes. Raleigh brakes are extremely efficient, and for all ordinary purposes the rear brake is amply powerful enough to bring the machine to a standstill in a short distance. As far as the new rider is concerned, it is better not to use the front brake unless the road is perfectly dry and there is no fear of side-slip.

"Running-in." Before being assembled in the machine, every engine is tested on a bench at the works; it is then again tested, after assembling, on the road and, unless these two rigorous tests are satisfactorily passed, it is not sent out to the agent. But, in spite of these two tests, the engine is not yet what is termed properly "run in." After an engine has run the equivalent of about 500 miles of normal use, the surfaces of the bearings acquire a glass-like surface of extreme hardness.

If an engine is raced during the first few weeks of its life, small abrasions will be made on the surface of the bearings. It is therefore essential, if the engine is to enjoy a long life, that it should not be unduly hustled until it has run at least 200 miles. This may seem rather a hardship on the man who has just bought a super-sports model and wants to put her through her paces immediately, but an engine well and thoroughly run in in the first place will outlast one that has been carelessly handled during the first few weeks of its life.

Lubrication. The correct setting for the sight feed control will be found by experience. With the larger models, the engine should be run lightly with the machine on the stand until oil flows from back feed pipe into oil tank. To check this, remove the oil filler cap and watch oil flow.

On the older Raleighs, lubrication is by means of a drip-feed fed by a hand-pump, which should be set to deliver a pumpful of oil to the engine in about five miles of normal running.

Tyres. The correct care of tyres has an important relation to the life of the tyres, the life of the machine, and the comfort of the rider.

Tyres should be correctly inflated—neither too hard nor too soft. To judge the happy medium, there should be the slightest perceptible bulge where the tyre rests on the road surface. If the tyres are too hard, the rider and machine will be unnecessarily jarred; if they are too soft, the walls or sides of the tyres will soon wear out. There is also the danger with soft tyres of stones and potholes denting the rims.

DRIVING A COMBINATION

The driving and engine control of a combination do not, of course, differ from that of a solo machine, and therefore the actual driving instructions need not be repeated here. But it is with the question of balance that the solo rider meets difficulty when he first attempts to drive a sidecar outfit.

A solo machine is steered by balance—its weight, in fact, almost making it balance and steer itself—but a sidecar combination must be steered by the handlebar, almost like a car. The solo rider who tries a combination for the first time must take great care of this, and it will be quite a little time before he is able to gain complete mastery over the machine. For a novice, it is not so difficult, for he has not got to " unlearn " the art of steering by balance.

Left-hand Corners. Owing to the centre of gravity of a combination being well over to the right—the machine being

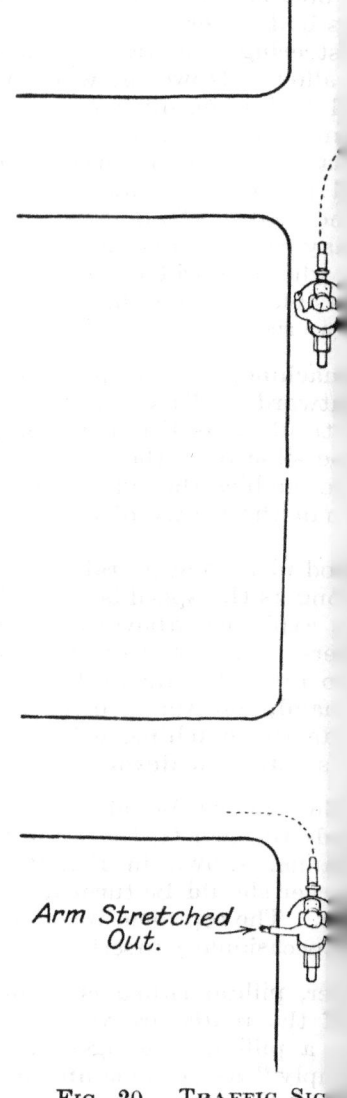

Arm Stretched Out.

Fig. 20.—Traffic Sig

DRIVING

a hill, or at any other time when the engine has to labour at all, it should be retarded.

Knocking. The curious sound known as " knocking " occurs in an engine when it is temporarily overloaded, such as on hill-climbing work. Knocking is a decided strain on the engine, and immediately it occurs, steps should be taken to prevent it by slightly closing the air lever ; if this is ineffective, the ignition lever should be slightly retarded. If these two movements fail to stop the knock, the machine should be put into a lower gear.

Hill-climbing. One often hears riders boastfully telling tales of steep hills in the district which they claim to have climbed on top gear. While this may to a certain extent be a meritorious performance in an official trial, it is certainly a foolish practice for the general rider. To make a machine struggle up a steep hill on top gear, knocking wildly and heavily labouring, is bad for the engine and invariably denotes a bad rider. The gearbox is provided for use and the novice need not feel it is a disgrace to drop into second gear immediately the engine begins to labour. In this way he will lengthen the life of his engine immeasurably and, incidentally, climb the hill more quickly. The power of an engine depends on the number as well as the power of the explosions in its cylinder. This power increases with its speed in a far greater proportion than the actual speed ratio, up to a certain speed. Therefore dropping into second gear will usually increase the speed of the machine, owing to the greater power put out by the engine. When descending a steep hill, use the brakes alternately, if possible, to prevent excessive heat on rear brake.

Brakes. Raleigh brakes are extremely efficient, and for all ordinary purposes the rear brake is amply powerful enough to bring the machine to a standstill in a short distance. As far as the new rider is concerned, it is better not to use the front brake unless the road is perfectly dry and there is no fear of side-slip.

" Running-in." Before being assembled in the machine, every engine is tested on a bench at the works ; it is then again tested, after assembling, on the road and, unless these two rigorous tests are satisfactorily passed, it is not sent out to the agent. But, in spite of these two tests, the engine is not yet what is termed properly " run in." After an engine has run the equivalent of about 500 miles of normal use, the surfaces of the bearings acquire a glass-like surface of extreme hardness.

If an engine is raced during the first few weeks of its life, small abrasions will be made on the surface of the bearings. It is therefore essential, if the engine is to enjoy a long life, that it should not be unduly hustled until it has run at least 200 miles. This may seem rather a hardship on the man who has just bought a super-sports model and wants to put her through her paces immediately, but an engine well and thoroughly run in in the first place will outlast one that has been carelessly handled during the first few weeks of its life.

Lubrication. The correct setting for the sight feed control will be found by experience. With the larger models, the engine should be run lightly with the machine on the stand until oil flows from back feed pipe into oil tank. To check this, remove the oil filler cap and watch oil flow.

On the older Raleighs, lubrication is by means of a drip-feed fed by a hand-pump, which should be set to deliver a pumpful of oil to the engine in about five miles of normal running.

Tyres. The correct care of tyres has an important relation to the life of the tyres, the life of the machine, and the comfort of the rider.

Tyres should be correctly inflated—neither too hard nor too soft. To judge the happy medium, there should be the slightest perceptible bulge where the tyre rests on the road surface. If the tyres are too hard, the rider and machine will be unnecessarily jarred ; if they are too soft, the walls or sides of the tyres will soon wear out. There is also the danger with soft tyres of stones and potholes denting the rims.

DRIVING A COMBINATION

The driving and engine control of a combination do not, of course, differ from that of a solo machine, and therefore the actual driving instructions need not be repeated here. But it is with the question of balance that the solo rider meets difficulty when he first attempts to drive a sidecar outfit.

A solo machine is steered by balance—its weight, in fact, almost making it balance and steer itself—but a sidecar combination must be steered by the handlebar, almost like a car. The solo rider who tries a combination for the first time must take great care of this, and it will be quite a little time before he is able to gain complete mastery over the machine. For a novice, it is not so difficult, for he has not got to " unlearn " the art of steering by balance.

Left-hand Corners. Owing to the centre of gravity of a combination being well over to the right—the machine being

DRIVING

considerably heavier than the sidecar, of course—on a left-hand turn, centrifugal force will tend to upset the balance. This is particularly the case when the sidecar is empty.

Should a new rider, when turning a left-hand corner, feel that his sidecar wheel has lifted off the ground—a sensation which thoroughly " puts the wind up " one, as the saying is—it is best for him to declutch and throw his body over towards the sidecar and stop as quickly as possible, steering in a straight line if the bend and the amount of traffic allow. However, when a little more experience has been gained and sufficient nerve acquired, this lifting of the sidecar wheel may be cured by doing exactly the opposite to this: that is to say, the machine may be *accelerated*. The engine will then pull the machine forward, forcing the sidecar wheel on to the ground again. To do this requires a good deal of confidence, but it may save an awkward spill if the sidecar wheel lifts on a corner where considerations of traffic make the other alternative impossible. It is well, however, not to wait to experiment in this till a crisis arrives.

Turning Corners. On a solo machine, the machine should be leant inwards and the body outwards. This requires a little practice, but is well worth the trouble, as this position places the centre of gravity as far as possible over the tyres' point of contact with the ground. It also enables the sides of the tyres —which are usually less worn than the centre of the tread—to obtain a firmer grip of the road.

With a combination, it is a good idea to accelerate the engine slightly on a left-hand turn (so long as the speed is not sufficient to overturn the combination, as explained above) and to close the throttle on right-hand corners. In this way the acceleration of the machine will tend to make it pull itself round the left-hand corner; on the other hand, the weight of the sidecar, which wants to travel faster than the machine, will help on a right-hand corner if the engine is throttled down.

Traffic Signs. Warning should always be given to traffic following by a driver who intends to turn to the right or left, and should be given in the manner shown in Fig. 20. This diagram also shows the way a corner should be turned, the rider keeping well to his left in each case. The reprehensible practice of cutting off right-hand corners leads occasionally to serious accidents.

Pillion Riding. In dry weather, pillion riding is a comparatively harmless pastime; but if the roads are wet or greasy, great care must be exercised if a pillion passenger is carried. The passenger should sit as " limply " as possible and be asked not to " assist " by attempting to balance. If possible, some

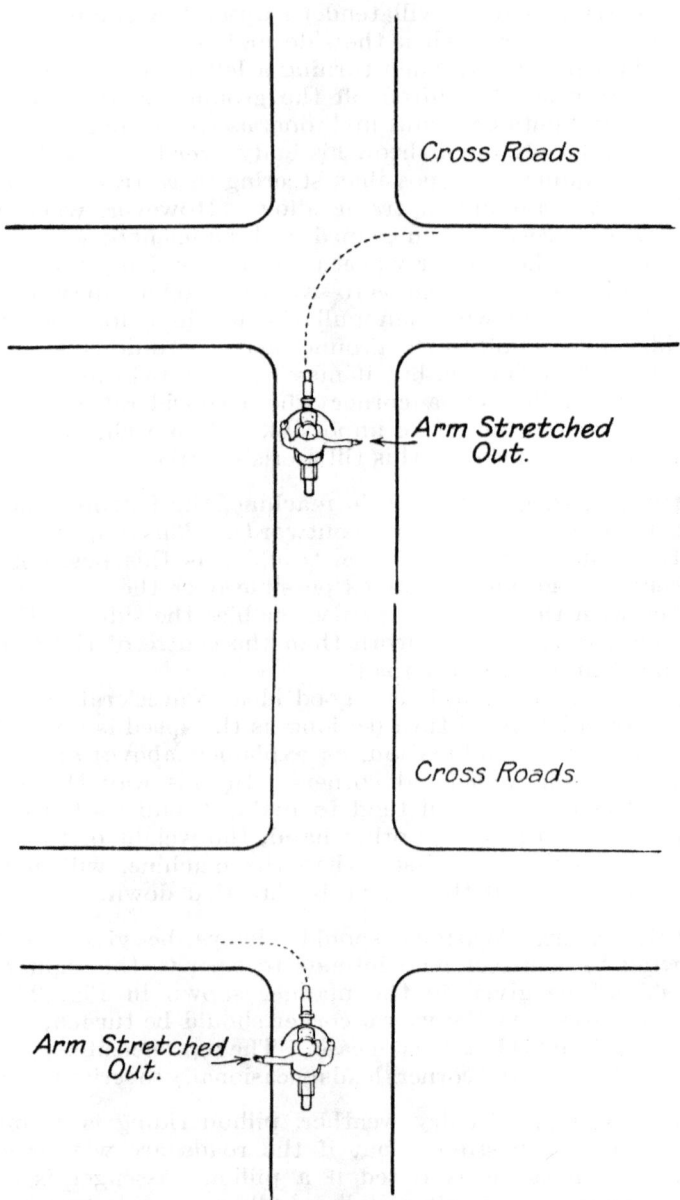

Fig. 20.—Traffic Signals to Use at Corners

DRIVING

sort of footrest should be obtained, so that the rider does not feel his pillion passenger swaying from side to side. As weight at the tail of the machine tends to cause side-slip, the pillion passenger should sit as closely as possible to the rider. The rider should remember that, at the best of times, riding on a carrier is one of the most uncomfortable things in the world, and so should go slowly over pot-holes and bad roads. A proper pillion seat, or at least a cushion, is a great asset, and, if the latter is used, it should be firmly strapped on to prevent its being thrown off, with the passenger, at an extra bad pot-hole.

RULES OF THE ROAD

Everybody must be aware of the rule of the road, which insists that drivers should keep to the left and should overtake on the right. Horses constitute an exception to this rule. They must be passed on the side on which they are led. Tramcars may be passed on either side. Certain towns have local by-laws relating to passing tramcars, and when in these towns the rider should watch the procedure of other traffic in relation to tramcars.

Traffic Driving. Riding in traffic demands a certain amount of patience, coupled with continual wideawakeness, the rider always being on the look-out for the quaint actions of some pedestrians and children. Remember, too, that the pedestrian has an equal right to the road with the motor-cyclist, although neither of them is allowed to make himself a hindrance or danger to the public at large.

When driving in thick traffic, the best plan is to keep up with the stream of traffic. The pushful rider who tries to forge ahead often comes to a bad end. It must be remembered that it is usually safest to jog along with the stream of traffic, seizing any advantages of openings that may occur in the traffic.

Stopping in Traffic. Temporary stops in traffic may be accomplished by de-clutching and pulling up with the brake, while the machine is supported by the rider taking one foot off the footrest. If one is held up for any length of time in a traffic block, it is wisest to move the lever into neutral position and to release the clutch lever. Keeping the machine in gear with the clutch out causes wear and friction in the clutch, with bad results. When stopping, hold out the hand as a warning to any vehicles behind, to avoid being run into, as their brakes may not be as efficient as yours are.

Skidding. Skidding is chiefly a matter of nerves; a jumpy rider will skid at the very sight of a cool rider ploughing his way steadily through grease. The way to avoid skids is to use a lower gear, thereby avoiding jerkiness of drive, and to keep as straight a course as possible. It is better to forge straight ahead through a sea of mud than to try to avoid it. Sudden application of the brakes or sudden accelerations and decelerations tend to make the driving wheel slip. Once it has begun to slip in one direction, it is free to slip and skid in any direction. Flat tyres are a constant source of skidding. To avoid skids, keep the tyres pumped up hard and drive with care, avoiding all sudden movements and all sudden swerves. To get out of a skid, slip the clutch at once and throttle down. The machine is then free-wheeling, and the skidding back wheel has a better chance of regaining its grip on the road. Never on any account use the front brake alone in skiddy weather. The front wheel is normally " free-wheeling," and for that reason front wheel skids are rare.

Animals on the Road. Cattle or sheep met on the road should be negotiated with great care. Cows frequently walk across the road at the psychological moment into the rider. As a consequence, they should be approached slowly. Horn-blowing has usually no effect bar frightening them and making matters worse ; it is usually better, and quicker in the end, to try and get round slowly before they quite realize what is the matter.

Night Riding. Riding at night requires a good lamp and plenty of warm clothing. A specially sharp look-out must be kept for unlighted objects in the road and for pedestrians. One of the chief troubles of night-riding is the glare from oncoming cars' headlights. So long as the light is not actually looked at, this glare will not cause a temporary blindness, and the rider should always keep his eye on the left side of the road, keeping well towards that side. If, however, the rider is troubled with the glare, it can be avoided by shutting one eye until the car has passed. Riding with only one eye open is hardly a practice to be recommended, but it is better than temporary blindness. When riding with only one eye open, keep a good look-out for vehicles ahead, as it is difficult to judge distances with only one eye.

Careful Driving. Roads are intended for the use of anybody who likes to make use of them, so that it should always be remembered that others have an equal right to them. Care in driving should be the keynote of every motor-cyclist, both for his own sake and for the sake of other road-users.

Other drivers, unfortunately, are not always as careful as

yourself, so that you must always be on the look-out for their wild antics which may cause accidents. It is to be hoped that you, kind reader, will never be involved in a serious accident; but if ever it comes to the point where an accident is inevitable, be a man and do your utmost to reduce the total damage to a minimum, even if it means taking a larger share of it yourself.

Confidence. After a week or so riding, the novice may acquire a certain confidence which will tend to give him the feeling that he is an expert rider. Every rider has this stage, which is usually abruptly terminated by a narrow escape from an accident, which brings the rider " back to earth " and makes him realize that care is still needed.

CHAPTER V

ROADSIDE REPAIRS

POSSIBLE troubles and their cures—Hints for roadside repairs and temporary means of getting home.

TROUBLES come to us in all walks of life, and in the early days of motor-cycling, attending to troubles was, of course, the chief feature—if not the attraction—of the hobby. But with the modern motor-cycle troubles are reduced to a minimum, and the veriest novice can safely sally forth to-day and reasonably expect to keep his appointment. Probably the chief trouble which comes to the modern motor-cyclist is a puncture; these certainly form the most numerous of troubles, although, luckily, probably amongst the easiest to put right.

PUNCTURES

Prevention being better than cure, it is usually helpful to fit a puncture preventer on a motor-cycle in the form of a piece of copper wire or chain arranged across the front and rear stands about half an inch from the tyre. This little device will often catch nails and pull them out of the cover. A nail does not usually penetrate right through the cover when the wheel first picks it up; normally, it just sticks in the cover the first time, and is then pressed home by each subsequent revolution of the wheel. A nail catcher will often pull it out before real damage has been done.

In mending punctures, extreme cleanliness of the tube and the cover is essential, as a layer of dirt between the patch and the tube will prevent their sticking together. When the puncture is noticed, the machine should be stopped immediately, as running on a flat or partially-deflated tyre will cause the tube to be nipped between the rim and the road, making the tube perhaps beyond all repair. If the puncture takes place when turning a corner, it may be necessary to slip the clutch to avoid a skid, in which case the machine should not be brought to a standstill by its brake.

The machine should be put on the stand, and on the front stand as well, if it is a front wheel puncture, and the cover carefully gone over to see signs of the point where the puncture has occurred. There may be a nail sticking in it, or a deep cut, or some other sign which will show the exact spot where the trouble lies.

ROADSIDE REPAIRS

If it is desired to remove the rear wheel, it should be done as shown in Fig. 21. The valve parts should be removed and the tyre deflated before attempting to remove the cover. It is well to examine the valve before removing the cover, if there is no apparent reason for a puncture. There may be a fault in the valve which may be the root of the trouble. If you do not suspect the valve, it may yet be well to replace and to pump up

FIG. 21.—HOW TO REMOVE THE REAR WHEEL

the tyre. Then, by moistening the finger and applying it to the valve air inlet, it will be possible to detect any leakage.

If no leakage can be detected, it will be necessary to remove the valve again and to take off the cover. Most covers are marked on the side which should be removed and this side should be eased off with tyre levers. It is best to commence operations at the point opposite the valve by inserting a tyre lever between the rim of the wheel and the edge of the cover. Two levers should be inserted about 6 in. apart and depressed, so that the edge of the cover is raised over the rim of the wheel. When a third lever is inserted on either side of the other two, the middle one may be removed and the process repeated. Then the tube may be removed just for about 10 or 12 in. each side of the puncture ; there is usually no need to take it out all the way round the cover.

The tube should be cleaned with sandpaper, or whatever is supplied for this purpose in the puncture outfit. The rubber solution, after being applied to the patch and to the tube round the hole, should be left at least five minutes to dry before being stuck on the tube. Smoke a cigarette, or go for a five minutes' stroll, while it is drying, to ensure that it gets thoroughly dry. The word " tacky," so beloved of puncture-outfit manufacturers, is rather misleading, for if a patch is applied while in this state, instead of being dry, it will probably not adhere. If time allows, it is even better to apply two coats of rubber solution, allowing each coat to dry thoroughly before applying the patch.

Before being replaced in the cover, the patch should be covered with a liberal sprinkling of French chalk, to prevent the tube sticking to the cover, and should be partially inflated to prevent its being nipped between the cover and the rim.

ENGINE TROUBLES

The class of troubles which come next in order to annoy the rider is engine stoppages. Once found, of course, the trouble can usually be quickly remedied ; and so, therefore, the chief asset for the novice is some rational system whereby he can quickly lay his hands on any likely trouble that may have caused his engine to stop. To frantically search hither and thither on no fixed principle is next to useless.

The essentials to the proper working of an engine are: (1) the mechanical completeness of the engine proper (nothing fractured) ; (2) an adequate supply of petrol vapour ; and (3) a spark to ignite this vapour. Troubles are usually connected with items (2) and (3).

Tracing the Trouble. We will suppose that an engine has stopped, or will not start ; the following tests should be made in the order they are given: Supposing the engine fails on Test 1, then turn to Trouble 1, later in this chapter, and apply the remedy. If it fails on Test 2, turn to Trouble 2 ; and so on. If it passes Test 1 satisfactorily, then carry on through the tests until it fails on one of them.

TEST 1. Make sure that the petrol level in the tank is sufficient to enable it to pass into the carburettor (unless the machine is standing facing downhill). A few drops should be run on the hand to make sure that it is petrol and not water.

ROADSIDE REPAIRS

TEST 2. Stand on kick-starter. The compression should be noticed—it should be sufficient to support the weight of the rider for a few moments. Successful passing of this test shows that the engine is in order mechanically, that is to say, that the cylinder, piston, valves, valve springs and valve timing are all as they should be.

TEST 3. Attempt to start engine with kick-starter. This test will probably fail, and its failing will show the cause of the trouble. If it is impossible to get the engine to fire at all, the rider knows at once that the fault lies in the ignition. If the engine fires three or four times and then stops, the rider knows that the ignition is all in order, and that it is the carburation that is at fault.

By this time the rider knows approximately where the trouble lies, and so is in a fair way of knowing how to cure it.

TROUBLES AND CURES

Section 1. If the engine fails on Test 1, then trouble may be easily remedied by refilling the tank with petrol. It should be made sure that it is petrol which is in the tank and not water or paraffin. An engine will not start from cold on paraffin, but will if engine is hot. Its use is not advisable, however.

Section 2. Failure on Test 2 points to trouble at one of the following points. The cure for each trouble is given at the same time as the malady. If the engine can be turned over quietly, without any mechanical noise which denotes fracture or a broken part, the trouble is probably one of the following items—

Broken Valve Spring. A spare valve spring should always be carried, but should the rider get caught out without a spare, it may be possible for him to get home by inserting a large nut between the base of the broken spring and the cotter pin, which will shorten the spring and, at any rate, enable the rider to get to the next garage. Care must be taken to see that ample room is left for movement of the valve and tappet, to prevent jambing and consequent fracture. If the spare spring is kept compressed by loops of wire or string it may be more easily fitted in place. This can be done by compressing it in a vice and tying with wire.

Broken Valve. A spare valve is a useful accessory which should be carried. It is better to carry an exhaust valve, as this is interchangeable with the inlet valve and can be used for either. On the touring models, the valves are of the same metal; but on the sports model, a special steel is used for the exhaust valve. Should the rider have no spare valve with him, a temporary remedy may be worked by putting the good valve on the exhaust (if it is the exhaust valve which has broken), and the inlet valve will then have to act as an automatic valve. This can only be done when the valve breaks at the bottom where the cotter pin is inserted. A very light spring can be made from wire and coiled round the valve. The suction of the engine will open the valve at the correct moment, while the light spring aids its closing without being too strong to overcome the suction of the engine. If, however, the valve has snapped off at the top, nothing can be done but to push the machine to the nearest garage.

Valve-timing Deranged. If this is the case, it should be put right, the valve timing being set again as in the instructions given in the following chapter. This is not a trouble likely to occur on the road.

If strange noises emanate from the engine on its being turned, trouble may be looked for in the following items—

Valve Cotter Broken. This may or may not cause noise, but is easily seen if it is the cause of the trouble, owing to the valve spring falling down on to the valve guide. If near a garage, a new cotter pin can be obtained, but in emergency a short nail would serve the purpose for a short distance; but a cotter pin should be obtained at the first garage, as the pressure of the valve spring will bend almost any nail and make it difficult to extract from the valve stem.

Broken Piston. If this is suspected, the engine should not be turned at all, as the sharp edges will score the cylinder walls and do damage if the pieces of the piston fall into the crankcase. The only remedy is to push the machine, in neutral gear, either home or to the nearest garage for a new piston to be fitted.

Broken Gudgeon Pin. The same as for broken piston applies; the engine should not be turned at all, and a new pin obtained at once.

Broken Connecting Rod. This and the last two items are, happily, of rare occurrence, but the same remarks apply—the engine must not be turned, and a new part should be obtained at once.

Section 3. This test shows us whether the trouble is with carburettor or with ignition.

If it is a carburettor trouble, then the following items should be systematically examined and, if trouble is found at any one of them, it can be duly remedied.

Air Vent in Tank Choked. The small pin-hole in the filler-cap may become blocked with dust and dirt, causing a vacuum in the tank, so that the petrol cannot flow down the pipe to the carburettor. The air vent should be cleaned out with a pin and the filler replaced.

Needle of Float Sticking. This may be due to the needle being bent or dirt accumulating. In the latter case, remedy is obvious; but if needle is bent, the rider may try and straighten this, but it is usually a difficult task, which requires expert assistance.

Jet Choked. The jet may be removed by unscrewing the nut underneath it; the jet may then be screwed out of its holder and cleaned by blowing and by running petrol through it from the priming tap. If this fails to dislodge the dirt, it may be cleared with a very fine wire, but care should be taken in doing this not to enlarge the bore of the jet.

Air-lock in Petrol Pipe. This does not often happen with the Raleigh, owing to the petrol pipe being curled in such a way that an air-lock is not likely to occur. The cure is to remove the petrol pipe completely and re-fix it, when the air-lock will probably have disappeared.

No Petrol in Tank. Remedy obvious, if near a garage or other supply of petrol. If, however, neither is available, a passing motor-cyclist must be hailed. He will probably not have a spare tin; but if he is willing to part with some out of his tank, it may be transferred by means of the rubber bulb of the horn used either as a suction syringe or as a receptacle to catch the petrol from the priming tap.

Petrol Not Turned On. Remedy obvious.

Choked Petrol Pipe. It should be unscrewed at both ends and blown clear of matter, care being taken to avoid water getting into it.

Air Leak. Probably denotes that attachment of the carburettor to the cylinder has worked loose, in which case it should be tightened. If the leak is due to a fracture, it may be repaired temporarily with insulating tape, or, if available, soap makes a fine caulking material.

Wrong Setting of Carburettor Levers. For starting, normally speaking, the petrol lever should be about one-third open and the air lever closed. All engines have different whims for settings, and experience is the best guide to these positions.

Closed Throttle—Controls Failing to Work. This will be caused either by the control wires breaking or stretching, or by the slides in the carburettor sticking, owing to dirt. Dirt may be easily cleaned off; the slides should not be oiled, as this only collects dust and repeats the trouble later on, but they can be rubbed with graphite if they will not slide sufficiently easily. A broken control wire is usually difficult to repair on the road. If it is the air slide wire which has broken, pull off the Bowden wire covering and open the air slide half-way, keeping it open by twisting the Bowden wire round a convenient part of the frame. This enables the rider to struggle home, controlling speed roughly by the throttle. If, on the other hand, it is the throttle wire which has broken—which is more usually the case—the wire may be transferred from the air slide to the petrol slide. This will enable the throttle to be worked, while the air slide is jambed open as before.

IGNITION TROUBLES

Weak Spark. Is probably due to the plug points being too far apart, in which case they should be knocked gently closer together. The correct distance is $\frac{1}{32}$nd of an inch, slightly thicker than the gauge on the magneto spanner, or the thickness of a visiting card.

Incorrect Timing. To ascertain the approximate timing, the compression tap should be removed and a stiff wire inserted, to ascertain when the piston is at the top dead centre of its stroke. The ignition lever should be retarded fully and, when the piston has reached the top dead centre of the compression stroke, the points of the contact breaker of the magneto should be just about to separate. (See Fig. 22.) Actually, the spark should occur when the piston reaches 8 mm. before top dead centre, when the ignition is fully advanced.

Magneto Timing Slipped. The sprocket which drives the magneto armature is held in place by a key on a taper shaft, and locked by a set-screw. If for any reason the magneto drive is disturbed, care should be taken when refitting to see that all is locked up securely; otherwise the sprocket may slip and timing be deranged.

Plug Oiled Up or Sooted. This denotes that the engine is

ROADSIDE REPAIRS

receiving too much oil, and therefore the oil supply should be checked and, if necessary, cut down; or else the mixture is too rich, in which case fit a smaller jet. The plug should be removed and cleaned with petrol and a brush, if available.

Plug Short-circuited. This is usually caused by an accumulation of soot up inside the plug, or by the plug points being too

FIG. 22.—THE CONTACT BREAKER OF THE MAGNETO
P = Contact Points

near together and bridged by an accumulation of carbon. Remedy: clean.

Weak Spark. May be due to the springs of the brush in the magneto being too weak, or the brushes worn. Whichever it is the faulty part should be renewed. To make starting more easy, the plug points should be put closer together. Or it may be due to a faulty sparking plug.

Contact Points Dirty or Worn. If the two platinum surfaces of the contact breaker are black or pitted, it is usually a sign that sparking has been taking place owing to the condenser having broken down. Repair of this is a job for the makers of the magneto. The points may, however, be cleaned by drawing two or three thicknesses of coarse brown paper through the gap.

Contact Breaker Rocker Arm Sticking. Clean with a brush dipped in petrol. This may also be due to fibre bush swelling, due to damp. If so, take it off and dry in oven or warm place.

H.T. Cable Detached or Perished. Remedy obvious.

Short Circuit. This may be due to oil having dropped on to the rubber insulation of the H.T. cable. If available, a new cable should be fitted, or temporarily the perished part may be wrapped round with insulating tape or a piece of rag.

Loose Contact Points. The points should be tightened up by means of the locking nuts with the magneto spanner supplied. The gap at its maximum opening should be approximately $\frac{1}{64}$th of an inch, which can be tested by the feeler gauge on the magneto spanner or a thin visiting card.

Broken Carbon Brushes. These should be renewed, or if no new ones are available, the old portions should be made to protrude as far as possible on to the ring. Any broken particles of brush should be carefully taken out, or they will score the surface of the ring or cause short-circuits. In emergency, a piece of " lead " from a pencil will serve as a brush, the wood being shaved down sufficiently. On a twin the remaining brush can be broken in two and half fitted to each.

Key of Contact Breaker Sheared. This is a most unlikely form of trouble, but if it occurs it can be temporarily put right, to enable one to get home, by replacing the key in its correct place on the shaft and screwing up the centre nut of the contact breaker. Be careful not to screw this too tightly.

Insulation of Magneto Broken Down. When the insulation of the windings has broken the repair is invariably a job for the makers and should not be attempted by the amateur.

OTHER TROUBLES

Other troubles may be encountered, such as—

Overheating. This may be due to a variety of causes, the usual cause being excessive carbon deposit on the piston and head of the cylinder. For this, of course, decarbonization, as explained in Chapter VI, is the only remedy. Under-oiling causes overheating, in which case the engine should be given a more generous supply of oil, after it has been allowed a rest by the wayside to cool down. The mixture may be too strong, owing to the gauze in the air inlet of the carburettor being coated with mud. The fish-tail on the straight-through type exhaust pipe may be clogged up. It is possible that the nut underneath the crankcase, used for draining purposes, may have come out, in which case a cork or piece of rag stuffed in its place will enable the rider to get home.

Wrong Tappet Adjustment. Tappets should be so adjusted (when engine is warm) that the inlet tappet has about four-thousandths of an inch clearance from the bottom of the valve stem, and the exhaust tappet at a very slightly greater distance, say six-thousandths. The reason for this clearance is that the metal expands on getting hot, and, were no clearance left, the valve would not properly close when hot. To adjust the tappet, hold the nut *A* in Fig. 23 firmly with a spanner and loosen nut *B*. Then it is possible to adjust nut *A* to the correct height by turning to right or left as required. Nut *A* should then be again firmly held and nut *B* tightened, so that the two are locked together.

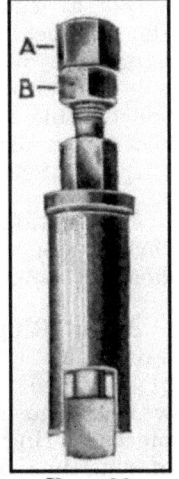

Fig. 23
Diagram Showing How to Adjust the Tappets

Lubrication Failure. The Raleigh mechanical oil pump is extremely reliable, owing to the fact that oil passes through all the moving parts of the pump, eliminating wear as much as possible. The most likely cause of trouble is dirt in the oil itself, which may block an oilway, in which case the afflicted part must be taken off and blown clear. The only likely cause of failure with the dry sump system will be through the clogging of the filters. The pump should be dismantled and the filters thoroughly cleaned with petrol.

Float Punctured. This, of course, causes the float to sink and to render the needle inoperative, thereby flooding the carburettor. The best cure for this trouble is to turn the petrol tap on just sufficiently to allow enough petrol to trickle through to supply the needs of the engine. On reaching home, the float should be taken out, all petrol shaken out of it, and thefloat put in the sun for all remaining petrol to evaporate. The puncture may usually be found by placing the float in water, when a stream of bubbles will indicate the spot. But if the puncture is too small for it to be found by this means, the float should be placed in hot water, which will expand the air inside the float and thus cause bubbles to betray the spot of the puncture, which should be marked immediately. For repair, the float should be taken to a jeweller to solder. It is too delicate a job for the amateur, or even the garage mechanic, to attempt successfully. Unless the jeweller is a motor-cyclist himself, it should be explained to him that the float has to float in petrol ; therefore as little solder as possible is required, and it may be advisable to put a spot of solder on the opposite side of the float to the puncture, so that the float can preserve its balance.

Valve Badly Pitted. The usual cause of this trouble is that either the exhaust lifter has been used too much, or that the valve tappet is adjusted too high. In either case, it means that burnt gases have played havoc with the surface. As mentioned above, at least four-thousandths of an inch should be left between the exhaust valve tappet and the base of the stem, to allow for expansion when hot. If this clearance is not left, the valve will be unable to sit on its seating when the engine is hot. If the trouble is through abuse of the exhaust lifter, the practice should be abandoned forthwith. The remedy is to grind in the valves. (See Chapter VI.)

Piston Rings Gummed Up. This is due to excessive oil causing carbon deposits. They should be taken off the grooves and cleaned, as explained in Chapter VI.

Piston Ring Broken. A broken piston ring can usually be traced by a peculiar squeak which it causes. It should be attended to at once, or the fractured edges will score the cylinder walls. The crankcase should be carefully inspected for broken pieces of ring and the cylinder not replaced until every particle of ring has been accounted for. As piston rings are made of cast iron, they usually break in one spot only, and therefore do not, as a rule, cause much damage.

Piston Ring Slots in Line. Although this will not cause an engine to stop, it will somewhat affect compression. The rings should always be placed with their slots on equidistant sides of the piston.

Cracked Gudgeon Pin. This is also of rare occurrence and, when it occurs, should be replaced by a new one.

Bad Compression. This may be due to a variety of causes; worn piston rings; replace with new rings, obtained from the manufacturers; the valves may need grinding in, the piston ring slots may be in line, the valve springs may be weak, the valves may be pitted, or the tappet clearance too small. The cures for these various faults have been already explained. The remaining causes are as follows—

Carbon Deposit. This will occur after about 2,000 miles of running, when the engine should be decarbonized, as explained in Chapter VI. It occasions pre-ignition, which robs the power stroke of much of its power. The fresh gases being sucked in, meet glowing ends of carbon which pre-ignite part of the new charge.

Wrong Timing. If the valve or magneto timing has been disturbed, they should be put right again, as shown in Chapter VI.

Cams Worn. This occurs only after years of wear, when the cams should be replaced by new ones.

Gear Too High. New machines which are sent out intended for solo work are fitted with a higher gear ratio than those used for combinations. Therefore it should be stated, when ordering, whether a solo or combination gear is required. A solo machine, on being attached to a sidecar, may have its gear ratio lowered by fitting an engine sprocket with one or two teeth less than that used for solo work.

Weak Valve Springs. Heat will cause a spring to lose its temper, in which case the spring should be replaced by a new one. When it is desired to test which of two springs is the stronger, they should be pressed against each other, the weaker spring, naturally, giving more than the other. If no new spring is available, the stronger spring should be used for the exhaust valve.

Water in Petrol. Water in small quantities will cause the engine to splutter, and in larger quantities may cause a complete stoppage. The best cure is a thorough one, namely, to empty the tank, mop up as much of the remaining moisture as possible with a rag tied on the end of a stick, and then leave the filler cap off until the water has completely dried up.

Sticking Valves. A sticking inlet valve causes popping in the carburettor, and a sticking exhaust valve explosions in the silencer.

Colour of Exhaust. Black smoke denotes too rich a mixture (more air needed); blue smoke denotes an excess of oil.

The above covers practically all the troubles which are likely to arise in motor-cycling. Many of them are extremely improbable; however, it is felt that they are all worth noting. They are given, therefore, at the risk of frightening the would-be motorcyclist, who may be staggered by the possible troubles which lie before him. But happily the modern motor-cycle is a most reliable machine.

CHAPTER VI

OVERHAULING—HINTS AND TIPS

DECARBONIZING—Systematical overhauling—Parts of the machine to watch for renovation.

AFTER a machine has been ridden 2,000 to 2,500 miles, a certain loss of power and a tendency to overheat will be noticed. This is due to the carbon deposit which has accumulated on the inside of the cylinder and on the piston. To enable the engine to regain its former efficiency, it is necessary to remove this excess of carbon.

There are two methods of doing this: one is by means of removing the cylinder, or cylinder head in the case of the O.H.V. sports model, and scraping off the carbon ; and the other method is termed the oxygen process. This latter process makes use of the fact that an oxygen flame consumes carbon ; the valve caps (or sparking plug in the case of the O.H.V.) are removed and a blowpipe is inserted through one of them, and twisted and turned inside the cylinder so that the flame consumes all the carbon. While this is certainly a very handy process for the man who has not the time or inclination to decarbonize by the old and longer method, it is doubtful whether it is so efficient, and is therefore not to be recommended if the rider has time to dismantle his engine.

The older and surer method of getting rid of the carbon is as follows, and does not take so long as it would seem from the description. The first time the amateur performs the task, he may take a day to do it ; but experience comes in time, and the whole job need not then take more than a hour or so. On the wonderful Raleigh round-the-coast run a year or two ago, the Raleigh twin belonging to Mr. Gibson was decarbonized, valves ground in, carburettor and sparking plugs cleaned by two men under official observation in just under the two hours, so that one man on a single-cylinder motor-cycle should not take much more than this time.

For convenience in working at the machine, it should be placed on the stand ; and if a platform can be arranged so that the machine is 2 ft. off the ground, a great deal of backache may be avoided. A box is also a very useful accessory into which all odd nuts, etc., can be placed as they are taken from the machine.

OVERHAULING—HINTS AND TIPS

The petrol should be turned off and the petrol pipe disconnected from the top of the carburettor. The bolt of the clip, which attaches the carburettor to the inlet pipe of the cylinder, should next be loosened, so that the carburettor may be taken off and allowed to hang loose on its control wires, supported meanwhile by a loop of string attached to the frame.

The compression tap, valve caps, and sparking plug should next be taken off and placed on one side. The exhaust pipe union must next be unscrewed. In some cases this may prove rather refractory, and if difficulty is encountered, one or two sharp taps with a hammer on the end of the spanner will probably loosen it. This is a right-hand thread, as in normal practice, that is to say, unscrews by turning the top or right-hand side towards you.

The four nuts which hold down the cylinder should then be taken off; in the case of the O.H.V. model, it is first necessary to remove the push rods, as shown in Fig. 24, and then the four bolts which connect the cylinder head and cylinder can be removed. For this purpose, the tappet spanner is used, and should be inserted between the second and third fins from the top. (See Fig. 25.) The engine should then be turned so that the piston is at the bottom of its stroke, and the cylinder can then be lifted off by being tilted either backwards or forwards.

A rag should be wrapped round the base of the piston to prevent dirt and carbon getting into the crankcase, and the carbon may then be scraped off the head of the piston with a chisel. Unless the piston rings are black or pitted, it is best to leave them undisturbed.

However, if there are signs of carbon accumulation underneath the rings, and it is desired to move the rings, they may be removed by getting three strips of springy metal, which should be slipped under the rings and evenly spaced, when the ring may be removed easily, as illustrated in Fig. 26. Remember that the rings are made of cast iron and are therefore extremely brittle, so that they must be handled with care.

Any carbon which has collected in the grooves of the piston should be carefully scraped out. The rings should have sufficient spring left in them to show a gap of about 4 mm.; and if they do not possess this, it is advisable to renew them, especially if they show signs of wear.

VALVE GRINDING

After all the carbon has been scraped from the inside of the cylinder head, the valves, if necessary, should be ground in. To do this, it is necessary to remove the valve cotter pins. A

Fig. 24.—How to Remove an O.H.V. Push-rod

Fig 25.—Removing Cylinder Head of the O.H.V. Engine
Note position of the spanner

special tool can be obtained of most garages, which is used to keep the valve springs compressed while the cotter pin at the base of the spring is removed from the slot in the valve stem.

The valve is provided with a slot in its head, so that a screwdriver may be inserted for grinding purposes. A little carborundum powder, or emery powder, should be obtained and mixed with paraffin into a paste, and smeared on the face of

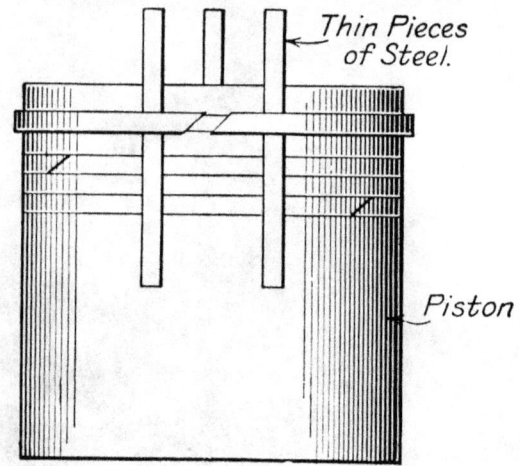

FIG. 26.—A SIMPLE METHOD OF REMOVING PISTON RINGS

the valve, or a ready-made valve grinding mixture should be bought in a tin for the purpose. The valve should then be dropped into place and rotated with medium pressure on the screwdriver for about ten minutes. Pressure should be released after every few turns and the valve turned to a fresh position on its seating, so that an even surface is obtained all the way round its face. After grinding and replacing the valves, carefully check the tappet clearance to four-thousandths of an inch.

Many riders prefer to send their valves to the works to be refaced instead of grinding them in themselves, and in many ways this is preferable. Fig. 27 shows how continual grinding in will wear away the cylinder seating as well as the valve itself; this wear is, of course, avoided by sending these valves to the factory to be refaced, which is done at a nominal charge.

RENEWING VALVE SPRINGS

Before the valves are replaced, the springs should be examined ; the exhaust valve spring, especially, is liable to lose its temper owing to the heat to which it is subjected, and may therefore need renewing, which will result in increased power. The spring should be sufficiently strong to enable it to resist being pressed down completely between the two hands with comfort.

THE GUDGEON PIN

The rider may want to remove the gudgeon pin for examination, and to do this it is necessary, in the case of engines fitted with cast-iron pistons, to remove the bolt through the connecting rod. The large holes in the sides of the piston are drilled so

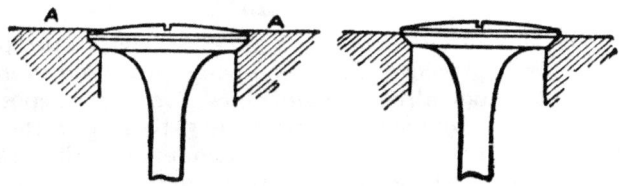

FIG. 27.—DIAGRAM SHOWING HOW TOO MUCH VALVE GRINDING WILL WEAR AWAY THE VALVE SEATING

that it is possible to get at this bolt. The bolt should be removed, and it is then possible to slip the gudgeon pin out of its place. After several thousand miles' running, wear may be noticeable at the ends of the pin and, if necessary, it can then be renewed. In exceptional cases, the piston may be worn, when it will be necessary to renew that as well as the pin.

In replacing the gudgeon pin, care must be taken to see that the bolt through the centre is carefully replaced, or trouble will result. The butt should be secured by a new locking washer and the gudgeon pin itself should be clamped tightly in the " little end " of the connecting rod, the bearing being taken by the ends of the gudgeon pin only.

On the later models, however, the gudgeon pin is not rigidly fixed to the connecting rod, but is fully floating, so that wear may be noticeable in the centre as well as at the ends. In this case, a new pin, complete with end-caps, is simply pushed into position.

CLEANING THE CRANKCASE

The drain-plug at the bottom of the crankcase should be removed, allowing the oil to drain out, and the crankcase then swilled out with paraffin. In replacing the plug, make sure that it is screwed up tightly, as its loss on the road would lead to serious results owing to loss of oil and consequent under-lubrication of the engine. With the dry sump lubricated models, the oil tank and sump should be emptied and washed out with *petrol*. The oil filters should also be thoroughly cleaned. When the petrol has had time to evaporate, replace the plugs and fill the tank with fresh oil. This should be repeated every two thousand miles, but the oil level should be kept at the correct height by constant additions.

This covers all the operations necessary during decarbonization of the engine, so that the engine may now be reassembled.

REASSEMBLING

The valves should be replaced in their respective pockets, and the cotter pins replaced while the springs are held compressed with the special tool already mentioned for this purpose.

To prevent oil leakage, it is necessary to renew the washer which was between the base of the cylinder and the crankcase. For this, a square of cartridge paper, or thick brown paper, should be procured. The cylinder should then be placed upside down on the bench and the square of paper laid on it. A light hammer should then be used, the paper being held firmly, and the paper tapped all the way round the base of the cylinder, so that the spigot will cut a neat circle of paper. This inner portion is then, of course, scrapped, and the paper washer will then fit round the base of the cylinder. When this is fitted, the paper should be again tapped with the hammer round the outside edge of the flange of the cylinder, so that it can be neatly torn away from the edge; if it is carefully tapped with the hammer, it will come away neatly all round the edge.

This, then, forms a neat washer, which will be oil-proof; and it should be examined to make sure that there are no tears or cracks in it before replacing the cylinder. It should then be soaked in linseed oil or engine oil before being placed finally in position.

The cylinder may next be replaced, or the cylinder head, if it is the O.H.V. sports model that is being operated upon, a new copper asbestos washer being obtained if the old one shows any signs of damage. The four holding-down nuts should be screwed on with the fingers, first of all. Then when all nuts are finger-tight, they should be screwed round half a turn with the special

Fig. 28.—View of the 3·48 h.p. Super-Sports Raleigh with Timing Gear, and Magneto Chain Cover Removed

spanner until all four are fully screwed up. It is most important that all the four nuts should be screwed up to exactly the same pitch. If one is not so tight as the rest, undue strain will be put on the cylinder, which may result in a cracked cylinder. The walls of the cylinder and the piston, inside and out, should be well smeared with engine oil before the cylinder is replaced in position.

TIMING GEAR

If it is found necessary to inspect the timing gear, this can be done by removing the magneto chain cover first and then the five screws which hold the timing gear cover in place. The timing pinions should be examined for slackness and play on their pins. The cams and valve rockers should also be looked at at the same time and, if badly worn, should be renewed, but this will be needed only after several thousands of miles of wear.

If the timing gear is dismantled at all, it may be easily replaced by noting the teeth of the gear-wheels which are marked. Fig. 28, on page 64, shows the timing gear of the 3·48 h.p. super-sports with the cover removed, and also shows the manner in which the marked teeth should be meshed. In some of the early engines sent out, the teeth were not thus marked, but the timing can be set by setting the cam pinion so that the inlet valve commences to open just as the piston reaches the top of the stroke. The correct timing of the inlet valve automatically times the opening and closing of the exhaust valve, since both valves are operated by the same cam.

The correct timing for the magneto can be found by fully retarding the advance and retard lever; the contact points of the magneto should be just on the point of separating when the piston is at top dead centre at the commencement of the firing stroke. If this has to be done, the compression tap can be removed and a piece of stout copper wire, or a straight hairpin, inserted to feel when the piston is at top dead centre.

GENERAL POINTS

There are many other points of the machine which should be systematically attended to from time to time. Most of these are points which can be looked over in the garage on a wet day, when much profitable time can be spent over the machine generally.

It is advisable to go over the tyres from time to time; any flints found embedded in the covers should be pulled out with a pair of sharp-nosed pliers; and if the gashes are of any considerable size, they should be filled up with the plastic preparations which most tyre manufacturers market for this purpose.

OVERHAULING—HINTS AND TIPS

Smaller gashes may be filled in with rubber solution ; but whether they are filled with rubber solution or the patent filling mixture, the tyres should be allowed twenty-four hours' rest before being taken out on the road, to allow time for setting firmly.

Tyres should be kept reasonably hard : they should show just the slightest perceptible bulge at the point of contact with the road. If they are softer than this, the machine will be inclined to roll, and considerable strain is set up on the walls of the tyres, which will weaken them in course of time and cause bursts. On the other hand, if the tyres are too hard, undue vibration is set up for the rider and machine, which is bad for both. The happy medium should be struck.

Magneto. The magneto needs little attention as it is sent out packed with sufficient lubricant to last a number of years ; it is best to leave it entirely alone. After a course of years, if the rider is doubtful that all is well with his magneto, it is far more satisfactory for him to return it to the maker for overhaul. The points of the contact breaker need adjusting from time to time. When apart, they should be adjusted with the magneto spanner until their distance apart is equal to the gauge.

Carburettor. The filter should be cleaned out periodically and the gauze brushed clean of any mud or dust that may have accumulated. Experiments can be tried with different sizes of jet to find out which gives most economical running. Remember that while a larger jet will give more power and speed when the engine is running fast, it is very wasteful and unsatisfactory when the engine is running slowly.

Crankcase and Gear-box. The drain plug at the bottom of the crankcase should be removed every 1,000 miles to allow the old oil to drain away. The crankcase should be replenished with five pumpsful of engine oil and the gear-box should be filled with a mixture of Speedwell " Crimsangere " and engine oil. Oil alone should not be used for the gear-box, as it is too light to cling to the teeth of the gear wheels effectively, and is inclined to work out of the box via the kick-starter and clutch. Pure grease, on the other hand, is too heavy, and tends to cling more to the sides of the box than to the gear wheels.

Lubrication. While on the subject of lubrication, the importance of using only first quality oils should be emphasized. The same grade and make of oil should be used wherever possible, but never mix a " mineral " oil with a " castor base " oil.

66   THE RALEIGH HANDBOOK

An essential feature is to buy the oil in sealed cans or in drums, so that the rider may be assured that he is getting the genuine article. It is fatal to go to a strange garage and accept anything brought out in a measure, for it may be a poor quality oil of low flashpoint, which may do more damage to the engine in 100 miles than in 10,000 miles of running on a first-class quality oil. The importance of using good oil cannot be over-emphasized.

Fig. 29 shows the various parts of the machine, apart from the engine, which need periodical oiling. About every 1,000 miles it is well to remove the spindle and cones, clean then, and pack them with a suitable hub grease. In the case of the 1925

Fig. 29.—The Important Parts of the Machine Requiring Lubrication

and later machines, the Enot's grease gun should be used. On machines fitted with internal expanding brakes, care should be taken not to use too much grease on the hub, as the surplus may get into the brake drums. When reassembling the wheels, the adjusting cones (those provided with flats to take the spanner) should be placed on the left-hand side of the wheel, the chain side of the machine. Before finally tightening the front hubs, make sure that the washers are exactly in their places in the recesses in the front fork, as this is necessary for them to retain their correct position.

Adjustment of Hubs. The hubs should always be kept carefully adjusted, so that there is no excessive side-to-side play or slackness in the wheel. On the other hand, the cones must not be so tight that they exert pressure on the ball bearings. When

OVERHAULING—HINTS AND TIPS

correctly adjusted, just the barest possible side-to-side play will be noticeable at the rim.

In chain-drive models, adjustment of the rear hub is carried out by means of the slotted collar between the outside brake plate and fork-end after the spindle nut on the same side of the wheel has been slackened. This collar is keyed to the hub cone, and is slotted to suit the special C-shaped spanner supplied in the tool-kit.

Lubrication of Head and Forks. When these are assembled, they are packed with sufficient grease to last at least 1,000 miles of running; after each 1,000 miles it is advisable to grease them with the grease gun, which is now supplied with all models. On the older models, which were not provided with the special nipples needed for this form of lubrication, thin oil should be used for lubrication through the oilers. An occasional clean out with paraffin is good, but the forks must be well soaked afterwards in oil or grease, as the case may be.

Speedometer. An almost indispensable accessory to economical running is a speedometer of reputable accuracy. A good make should be chosen, and it can be relied upon to give the rider much useful information regarding petrol and oil consumption and tyre mileage. It will point out to him whether his running is economical or not, and in the latter case will soon save its cost by enabling him to check his consumption and to put matters right.

The front spindle on the right-hand side of the wheel is made extra long to enable a speedometer to be easily fitted. No lubricant is needed in the instrument itself and wear is almost non-existent, and it is packed with the necessary lubricant when assembled. The shaft should be detached from time to time at the top end and a thick oil poured into it. Merely insert sufficient to lubricate: there is no need to fill the shaft completely with oil, as it will drain out in course of time and may get on to the tyres, with disastrous results.*

Care of Chains. The chains should be cleaned about every 1,000 miles by being soaked in paraffin and cleaned with a stiff brush. Graphite grease or "Crimsangere" may be applied to the front chain, which can then be replaced. This treatment, however, is not advisable for the rear chain, as grease will accumulate dust. In this case a dry lubricant, such as graphite, or one of the special chain lubricants, should be used.

* On the latest models a tank mounted speedometer can be supplied. This is driven from the gear-box, and receives its lubrication automatically.

After a chain has been run 500 miles, it will be found to have stretched slightly. This stretch, in the front chain, may be taken up by loosening the nuts which hold the gear-box in position and sliding the box back until the chain is of the correct

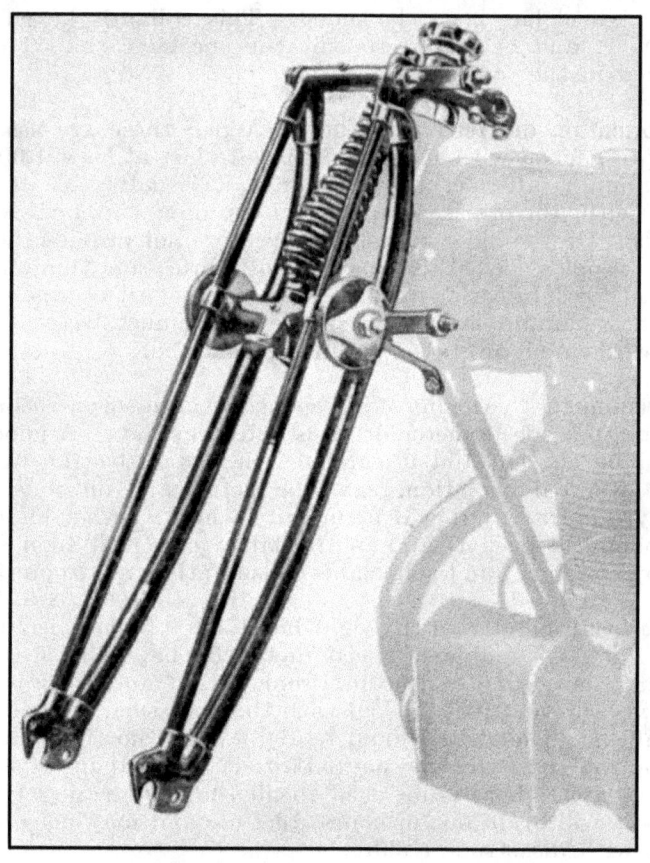

Fig. 30.—The Front Fork, Showing Nipples for Use with the Enot's Grease Gun System

tension. In the case of the rear chain, adjustment may be made by sliding the back wheel rearwards. The magneto drive may be adjusted by sliding the magneto platform forwards by loosening the two nuts on each side of the platform.

The correct tension of chains may be judged by feeling the

OVERHAULING—HINTS AND TIPS

up-and-down motion in the centre of their drive. The magneto chain may have about a quarter of an inch up-and-down play, the countershaft (front) chain slightly more, and the rear chain just over half an inch play. The sprockets should be turned to make sure that there is no tight spot anywhere in the chain.

Brakes. The moving parts of the brake levers should be lubricated periodically, but, of course, no lubricant should be

FIG. 31. SHOWING THE VERY ACCESSIBLE THUMB-SCREW ADJUSTMENT FOR THE REAR BRAKE

applied to the brake drums themselves. After a course of a year or more, brake lining may need renewing, and renewals may be obtained from the spare parts stockists mentioned at the end of this book.

Any movement of the wheels backwards or forwards may necessitate adjustment of the brakes, which should be done by means of the screw on the brake rod. Fig. 31 shows details of the rear brake adjustment. The length of the tie rod can be altered by rotating the small thumbscrew seen in the illustration. The machine should be placed on the stand, and the brake should then be adjusted by rotating the screw until the wheel rotates freely without touching the brake lining at any point.

Lubrication of Control Wires. Control wires, such as petrol and air controls, magneto control and clutch control, benefit from occasional lubrication. This is best done by smearing the ends with "Crimsangere" and inducing as much of it as possible to enter the sleeving. It is better, if time permits, to remove the wires entirely from their sleeving and clean them from rust, if necessary, and then replace after smearing them with "Crimsangere."

Lighting Sets. To get efficient service from a lighting set, it must be thoroughly clean and be kept in good order. To take acetylene sets first, the following points should be examined periodically—

The burners should be cleaned out occasionally with petrol, or by blowing them out with the tyre pump. If the burner continually chokes, fill the space in the tube underneath the burner with cotton-wool; this will hold up any foreign matter, and it can be renewed from time to time.

The inside of the generator should be thoroughly cleaned out each time it is refilled, no caked carbide being allowed to remain in it, as the dampness it holds will affect the fresh carbide. The rubber tubing should be periodically examined, and renewed when and where necessary.

It is usually more satisfactory to use a separate generator for each lamp, but if economy forbids this extravagance, care should be taken to see that each lamp gets only the pressure and the quantity of gas that it requires. A lamp which has too strong a pressure may have its supply cut down by wrapping copper wire round the tubing and thus lessening its diameter.

A Lighting Tip. We all of us, sooner or later, get caught out without a match in the world. In an emergency like this, if an odd piece of wire can be found (it is always useful to keep a piece of wire in the tool-bag for various purposes) an extension may be made from the magneto high-tension cable, and the lamp lit by sparks from the sparking-plug. Even if no wire is handy, the rider need not be thwarted. It is possible, but not easy, to obtain a light by holding the sparking-plug upside down and filling the space where the points are with petrol, causing a spark at the plug by rotating the kick-starter, and lighting a piece of paper from the burning petrol and thus lighting the lamp. This is, of course, hardly possible on a wet, windy night; but, although playing with fire is hardly to be recommended, it is decidedly better than riding in the dark or pushing the machine till one meets a person with a match.

Electric Lighting Sets. The chief item in an electric-lighting set which needs attention is the accumulator. The terminals of

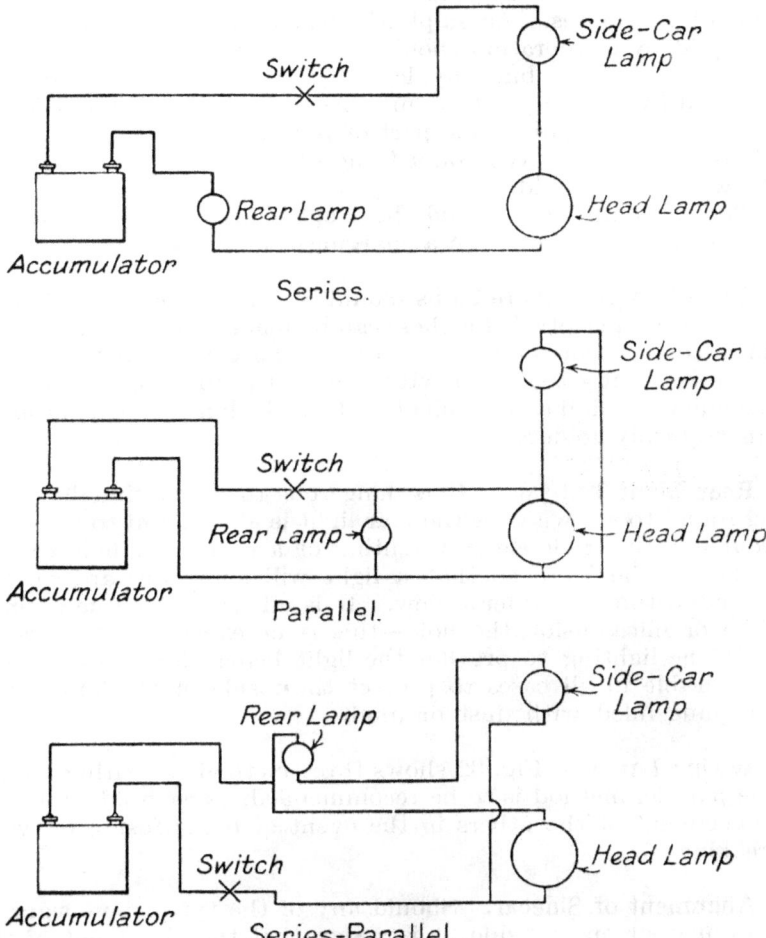

Fig 32.—Wiring Diagrams for Electric Lamps

this should be kept clean and free from corrosion by smearing them with vaseline. The diluted sulphuric acid with which they are filled should be kept about a quarter of an inch above the tops of the plates. As sulphuric acid does not evaporate, loss of liquid by evaporation should be remedied by filling with distilled water only, but any loss due to spilling over must be replaced by filling up with a mixture of sulphuric acid and water. The correct mixture is one part of pure acid to about five parts of distilled water. It is safer to add the acid to the water than the water to the acid.

The accumulator should be kept fully charged, and an occasional " touch-up " on a charging-board does it no harm.

Spare Lamps. Spare bulbs should be carried for electric lamps, and a useful receptacle for these can be made from a shaving-soap tin filled with cotton wool. They can be carried in the pocket (there is usually too much vibration in the tool-bag), or a little ingenuity will find a convenient spot on the lamp to which the tin can be firmly soldered.

Rear Light Tell-tale. It is dangerous to be continually turning round to see whether the rear light is alight, and to save this trouble with either electric lighting or acetylene, a hole can be drilled in the lamp so that a light will shine forward on the ground within the rider's view. It is advisable to glue a small piece of mica inside the hole—this is necessary in the case of acetylene lighting to prevent the light being blown out—and it is desirable in all cases to protect the inside of the lamp from becoming filled with dust or mud.

Wiring Lamps. Fig. 32 shows three methods of wiring lamps. The parallel method is to be recommended, as each lamp is then independent of the others in the event of bulbs fusing or wires breaking.

Alignment of Sidecar. Should any of the tyres show signs of uneven wear on one side, it is a sign that the alignment of the sidecar is at fault. This should then be remedied as shown in Fig. 33. The distances from A to C and B to D should then be exactly the same; that is to say, the wheels of the machine and the sidecar wheel should be running parallel.

Sparking Plugs. Lodge plugs are standardized on Raleigh machines, and the only attention they are likely to need will be periodical cleaning. This is best performed with petrol and a stiff brush. Fig. 34 shows the extent to which the plug should reach into the cylinder; and if other plugs are used, care should be taken to see that they do not under-reach or over-reach this distance, as either error will affect the compression ratio slightly.

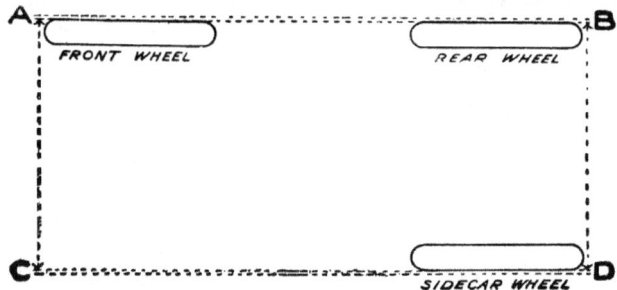

Fig. 33.—How to Align the Sidecar

In the case of over-reaching plugs, care must be taken to see that they are not long enough to foul the valve head. It is safest to keep to the plugs the makers choose.

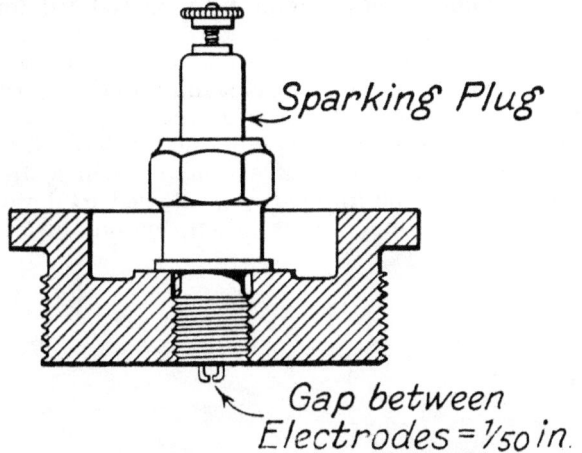

Fig. 34.—Diagram Illustrating Reach of Sparking Plug

Cleaning Machine. The eventual second-hand value of a machine will be greatly improved by careful and periodical cleaning. All moving parts should be kept cleaned and oiled to prevent grit working in and causing wear. Caked mud should be removed from the frame and mudguards, etc., by soaking it in water, or removing it with water from a hose-pipe ; it should never be scraped off, or the enamel will be scratched. Afterwards, it should be dried carefully and polished with a smooth cloth. Nothing looks worse than a rusty cylinder, and this can be improved by giving it a coat of boot-polish or lamp-black occasionally.

Re-enamelling. With so many excellent enamels on the market specially for this purpose, the amateur can obtain quite good results at enamelling while overhauling, if he desires. Naturally, no one can make a better job of it than the manufacturers, who have apparatus for stove-hardening the enamel ; and, if time allows, it is worth while sending the machine to them to have this done. However, if the amateur wishes to do it at home, the machine should be stripped of all fittings and the old enamel scraped off to the metal with an old knife, and then polished absolutely smooth and bright with emery cloth. All traces of the emery dust should then be removed with a non-fluffy rag and a coat of enamel applied. When this is thoroughly dried, it should be rubbed down with glass-paper and a second coat applied. The process should be repeated till four or five coats have been applied.

Dust is the great enemy of the enameller, and so the work should be performed where there is a minimum of dust to settle and the floor sprinkled with water frequently to lay the dust. Lining and crest transfers may be obtained if desired, and should be applied after the last coat of enamel. Then a final coat of special varnish should be applied and allowed to dry absolutely thoroughly before the machine is taken out on the road.

CHAPTER VII

SPEED WORK AND TRIAL RIDING

SPEED-WORK—Tuning a machine for speed and reliability trials—Trial-riding.

IF a machine is to be used for speed work, such as racing or exhaustive trials, it is essential that it should be tuned to the highest pitch of efficiency possible ; and therefore, before entering any event of this nature, the engine must be thoroughly decarbonized ; valves ground in ; and details, mentioned in the previous chapter, which need attention, put right.

The standard valve springs are amply strong enough for racing purposes and need not be replaced by stronger springs, unless any " valve bounce " is noticed.

As the Raleigh is fitted with an aluminium piston, little advantage is gained by interfering with it. But if the machine is an

1   2   3   4
FIG. 35.—PISTONS USED IN RALEIGH ENGINES
1. $2\frac{3}{4}$ Touring.   3. $3\frac{1}{2}$ S.V.
2. $2\frac{3}{4}$ O.H.V.   4. High compression (80 m.p.h.)

older model, fitted with a cast-iron piston, it is advisable to change it for an aluminium one, although this may necessitate rebalancing the engine.

The combustion head and valve ports should be made as smooth as possible, any rough edges being carefully eased off. Also valve stems, tappets, etc., should be carefully examined and high spots removed with an oilstone slip.

Experiments should be made with various size jets and the rider should use his judgment as to which jet is most suitable for the particular event.

The magneto timing for speed work is best found by experiment. The contact points should open when the piston is within 2 mm. of the top of its stroke and when the advance lever is fully retarded. This will be found to give the most suitable results.

COMPRESSION

For speed or trial work it is necessary that the compression be as perfect as possible. Tests should be made by smearing engine oil round the compression tap, round the valve caps and sparking plug with a brush, while the engine is running. Oil bubbles will betray any leak there may be, which, of course, should be remedied. Piston rings should fit as evenly as possible, and for short speed spurts it may be advisable to run with only one ring—the top one—in position, though for trial work it is better to keep to two rings, or oil will get above the one ring and cause too much carbon.

THE MAGNETO

This needs little attention before entering a trial, except that its driving chain should be examined for wear and slackness, and remedied if at fault. If the spring of the contact breaker is inclined to be weak, it should be replaced by a stronger one, as a slow make-and-break may cause misfiring. The platinum contacts of the make-and-break should fit with their faces absolutely square to each other, and be clean and bright. The sparking plug should be cleaned and set to the distance found most efficient; generally speaking, this will be found to be slightly less than $\frac{1}{32}$nd of an inch.

THE CARBURETTOR

A tendency to blowing back can be overcome by fitting a stronger inlet valve spring. The various filters should be cleaned out. Aviation spirit is recommended for use on special occasions, as this will vaporize more readily than any other. While benzole will give fair results for touring, it is not safe to use it if replenishments are to be made on the run, owing to the difficulty of ensuring that the fresh supply is of the same quality as that originally used. Benzole which gives excellent results on test in the garage may be unobtainable on the road. Benzole is slower in combustion and gives less detonating force, and is, therefore, not to be recommended for racing.

CHAINS

Chains should be used which have had their initial stretch taken out of them by 500 or 1,000 miles running. They should be thoroughly cleaned with paraffin or by being soaked in linseed oil before the run. The rear chain should be well rubbed with graphite. Chains should be adjusted to run easily, without undue slackness or tightness. They should be tested all the way round, as they may be tighter in one spot than in another.

BRAKES

Care should be taken that no friction is being set up by the brake rubbing its drum.

COMPETITION RIDING

Hitherto competition riding has been considered largely a matter for the trade rider, but to-day the amateur realizes he can purchase a machine of equal performance, and there is no reason why he should not equal the performance of the trade rider. In fact, in several cases in open competition amateurs have taken the premier awards. Success in a modern reliability trial depends primarily, of course, on the reliability of the engine and machine, which may be ensured as far as possible before the trial by attention to all the above tuning details. But an equally important factor in a trial is a cool head and concentration on the task in hand.

In speed events, the average amateur does not stand much chance against the professional trade rider; but for closed club events, or speed trials which are for amateurs only, it is worth while making the attempt.

But speed riding is no child's play; if the amateur intends to take it up, he must pay every attention before the event to get himself as well as his machine thoroughly tuned up. His nerves must be like steel; his wits must be ready to act the instant they are required, and he must practise, and keep on practising, until he is perfect at starting, as well as perfect at keeping up his speed.

Windage must be reduced to a minimum, and for this the clothing must be tight fitting. Leather clothing is desirable, to protect the rider in case of a spill. The rider must lay flat along the top tube and keep his knees pressed tight on his knee grips, to preserve balance and reduce windage to the minimum. Some riders steer by looking under the handlebar, but either this or above the handlebar will serve, so long as wind resistance—a large item at speed—is reduced. Fig. 36 shows the outlines of a rider sitting upright and one laying along the top tube. The former offers approximately $4\frac{1}{2}$ sq. ft. to the wind, whereas the latter offers 4, thus saving half a square foot in area. Wind pressure does not increase in direct proportion to the speed; it increases in proportion to the "square" of the speed. Thus, if it is a given pressure at 10 m.p.h., it is four times that pressure at 20 m.p.h., sixteen times at 40 m.p.h., and sixty-four times at 80 m.p.h. The importance of reducing windage is therefore obvious.

Do not make the fatal mistake of choosing too high a gear, which should be as low as practicable to reach the desired speed. The power of the engine depends on the number of revolutions, and anything which tends to reduce the revolutions will reduce the speed.

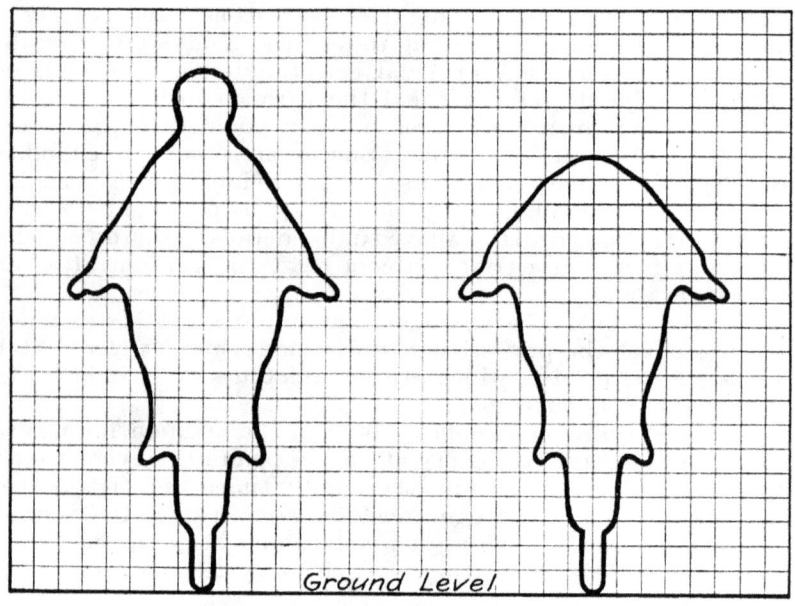

FIG. 36.—DIAGRAM ILLUSTRATING DIFFERENCE IN WIND RESISTANCE OFFERED BY UPRIGHT AND CROUCHING RIDERS

If it is allowed, it is wise to study the course and to practise on it beforehand. Discover how fine the corners may be cut, so that on the day of the race you are ready to take advantage of every foot of space and every fifth of a second. Always wear a crash helmet and Triplex goggles.

In cornering, lean the machine in and the body out; this method keeps the weight of the body over the point of contact between the tyre and the road.

The three essentials for speed work are: first-class tuning of engine, physical fitness and steel nerves on the part of the rider, of bursting and making the rest of the luggage in an incredible mess. Cigarettes should not be put in the suit case, or vibration will shake the tobacco entirely out of them in a surprisingly short time.

If the sidecar is provided with a locker, a small suit case or attaché case may be put in this, with oddments necessary for

Fig. 36a.—A Wayside Halt

one night. In this way, the " general " suit case may be left on the carrier overnight, and taken off every two or three days when replenishments are necessary.

An ex-Army groundsheet forms an excellent covering for the

TOURING

passenger can keep reasonably dry. The unfortunate motor-cyclist certainly does get wet, but will be none the worse for this if he can get a hot bath on arrival at his destination.

Dress. A man and his wife, or two friends, may travel in a combination, or on two solo machines, according to their inclinations, but in either case the question of dress must be carefully studied. Allowances have to be made for hot weather as well as rain, and one must start prepared for anything.

The golden rule is to start warm, especially the hands and feet, and, if possible, to keep warm. Therefore, for all-weather riding, a leather coat is a great boon and asset, or, failing this, a good trench coat which is absolutely waterproof. In wet weather, some riders prefer an oilskin and hat of the sou'-wester type, but these are rather uncomfortable to wear in dry weather. A good pair of rubber trench waders are very useful.

Bedford cord breeches, puttees or leggings, and good strong boots should be worn. A good thick cap, or a leather helmet, should be worn, and goggles are essential. The latter should be chosen with care and a pair obtained that fit accurately, or the resultant draughts will cause colds in the eyes. The plain glass goggles are dangerous to wear, in case of accident; and if the rider can afford a pair of Triplex goggles, with unsplinterable glass, he is well advised to do so. Failing this, the cheaper type, consisting of one large window of celluloid, is comfortable to wear and decidedly preferable to the glass type.

Luggage. The amount of luggage to be carried naturally depends on the length of the tour taken, and in any case it should be reduced to the minimum possible.

For a week-end tour, night attire is essential, a clean collar and handkerchief to correspond for each night away, spare shirt and vest, shaving tackle, tooth brush, brush and comb, soft hat, and socks.

For a tour lasting a week or more, the above items must be carried with a supply of underclothes, etc.; or if space is short, supplies may be posted to a spot midway on the tour, and soiled clothes then returned by post.

All luggage should be packed tightly to avoid damage from vibration and shocks, which on the carrier of a motor-cycle is no mean item. A Tan-Sad is a most useful accessory for saving luggage from vibration, or, failing this, a cushion between the luggage and the carrier will make a surprising difference. Bottles should be avoided, for fear of breakage, solidified toilet accessories in tins being more useful when touring. Tooth paste and shaving cream in tubes should not be taken, as these tubes have a habit

CHAPTER VIII

TOURING

DRESS—Luggage—Spare parts—Hotels—Economical touring—General hints.

FOR the man, and his wife, of moderate means, there is probably no more enjoyable holiday than a motor-cycle tour. For both, it has the freedom from cares of everyday life, which is one of the chief attractions of a holiday, and forms an enjoyable change of scenery which can never be given by the usual type of holiday —consisting of a fortnight at a seaside resort.

EXPENSES

The cost is not much more than a fortnight in one spot. Rooms at the seaside for two for a fortnight would probably cost, at the very least, £10; railway fares account for another £3; and outings and amusements, £4 or £5, giving a total of at least £17.

A motor-cycle tour of 1,000 miles, spread over a fortnight, on a 4·96 h.p. Raleigh combination, should not cost much more than this. The chief increase in expenditure is, of course, hotel bills; at small hotels of the "family and commercial" type the charge will be about 17s. 6d. to £1 per night for two for bed and breakfast, a total of between £12 5s. and £14; garage for the machine will cost about 1s. to 1s. 6d. per night, £1; petrol, at 75 m.p.g., at 1s. 6d. per gallon, about £1; lunches and food for the road, as mentioned below, 5s. to 7s. 6d. per day, £5; and money for sightseeing and odd expenses, £4. This gives a total of about £24.

By staying at smaller hotels (or with relations, if they are conveniently dotted about the country) this amount will be considerably reduced; and with strict economy it could be cut down to the level of the cost of a seaside fortnight.

But against the extra cost there is the advantage of the continually-changing scenery, the chance of seeing the country and its many places of interest, the health gained through being in the fresh air all day.

If the financial side of a trip such as this can be managed, an opportunity for a pleasant holiday is open for all who own motor-cycles. One has to chance wet weather, but the same thing applies to a seaside holiday; and in a modern sidecar, fitted with windscreen and weatherproof apron, the sidecar

SPEED WORK AND TRIAL RIDING

and a good start. The good start is the point usually neglected by the novice, but he should always bear in mind that most races are won at the start.

RELIABILITY TRIALS

Reliability-trial riding calls more for a cool head, confidence in oneself, and attention to *every* detail, however trivial. The usual procedure in these trials is for the rider to be checked, openly and secretly; and to gain his gold medal he must keep at a steady 20 miles per hour throughout the run, up hill and down dale.

A stop-watch, correct to a fifth of a second, and an expert knowledge of the route, gained by going over the course beforehand, if allowed, will help considerably. If the rider is driving a combination, a passenger who is cool and capable enough to keep one eye on the watch and the other on the speedometer *all* the time is a great asset.

One of the chief assets in a trial of this kind is to go one's own way and disregard the rest of the competitors entirely. Before the start, go carefully over your machine to make sure that everything is in first-class trim—even if other riders think it is a sign of your being " windy," ignore them—they will think differently later.

The route card on a trial may be carried fastened to the lamp generator with two rubber bands. But as vibration in this place often renders it unreadable, it is usually a better plan to fasten it on one's arm with bands. Another useful tip for carrying spare valve springs is to carry them already compressed by being bound with three pieces of fine wire. Then, if necessary, they can be slipped into place without the use of any special tools.

If the trial is secretly checked, an unswerving 20 miles per hour is essential; but if all the checks are open, a little time may be gained to leave some spare in hand for punctures or other emergencies. If you arrive at a check with a crowd of other riders, when your turn comes to sign the checking sheet, or whatever may be needed, see that the marshal puts down the actual time of your arrival, if this is to your advantage, and not at the moment when he records it. A little weakness or carelessness here may cost you your gold medal.

suit case, being dust and waterproof, and can be obtained for a shilling or so.

Legshields and Windscreens. An added comfort for touring can be obtained in the form of leg-shields and a handlebar windscreen, which will protect the rider from dust and rain.

Spare Petrol Tin. When carrying a spare petrol tin on the carrier, take care to pack plenty of cloth between tin and carrier

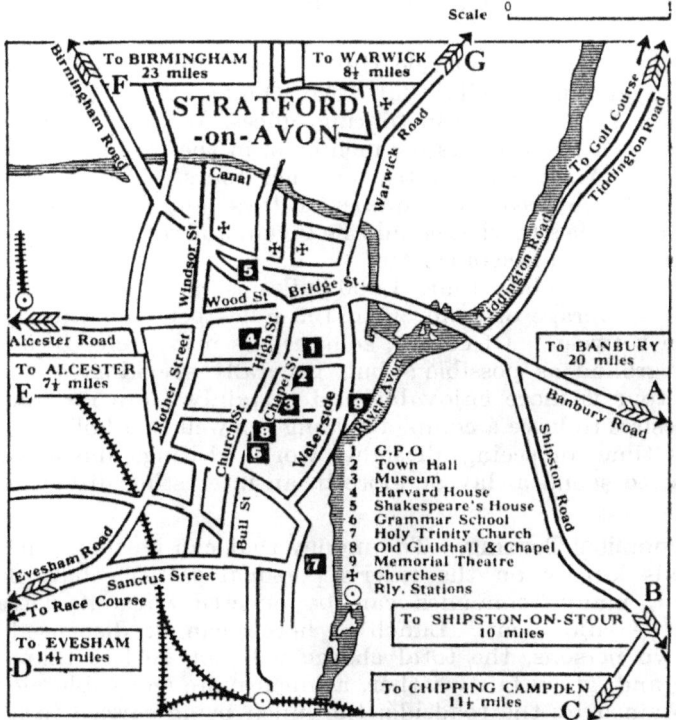

FIG. 37.—SPECIMEN MAP FROM THE DUNLOP GUIDE

to avoid abrasion and the discovery that all the petrol has disappeared when wanted.

Hotels. For any tour which is to be made during the holiday season, it is worth the trouble of booking rooms at the various hotels *en route*. Booking costs nothing but the stamp for the letter, and gives the tourists the comfort of knowing that there is a room waiting for them at the end of the day's run.

If the tourist cannot book ahead by post, telephoning during the day from A.A. roadside boxes will ensure for members a room for the night.

Choosing hotels in towns which the rider does not know is made an easy matter by consulting the A.A. Handbook, the A.C.U. Handbook, the Dunlop Guide, or the Michelin Guide. Each of these four books gives a list of reliable hotels, with their tariff charges, and a list of motor-cycle agents and repairers.

The Dunlop Guide and Michelin Guide also give reliable town plans, which are exceedingly useful in finding one's way through unfamiliar towns. Fig. 37 is a specimen map from the Dunlop Guide.

Routes. The Auto-Cycle Union, the Automobile Association, the Royal Automobile Club, the Dunlop Tyre Co., and the Michelin Tyre Co. all run touring offices, and will be pleased to supply *bona-fide* tourists (or members, in the case of the R.A.C., A.C.U. or A.A.) with routes for their tours. The approximate miles to be covered, the number of days, and the district which the rider wishes to visit should be given, and a full detailed route can be obtained free of charge.

For a fortnight's tour, 1,000 miles is quite sufficient. This gives an average of from 80 to 100 miles per day, with a day's rest in between. Of course, some riders may prefer to cover as much ground as possible ; but, generally speaking, a " pottering " tour is more enjoyable and certainly more restful, when one desires to have a complete change as well as a holiday. This allows time for seeing all sights worth visiting, and allows the tourist to spend a day or more in an interesting district should he desire.

Economical Touring. The money that can be spent on a tour depends largely on the rider's personal tastes ; but, if it is desired, many economies can be effected without detracting from the enjoyment. Lunch at hotels can be dispensed with. For two persons, the total charge will not be less than about 10s. ; and, given fair weather, a much more enjoyable meal can be obtained by the roadside, the lunch being carried in a small attaché case in the locker or foot of the sidecar. The sidecar occupant can do the shopping of a morning, while the other rider is filling up with petrol and oil, and generally getting the machine trim, when all the necessaries for a wayside picnic can be obtained at a fraction of the cost of a hotel lunch—and what is more enjoyable than this quiet wayside lunch, " far from the madding crowd," at the first delightful spot after mid-day ?

A good breakfast before starting is essential, especially in cold weather ; and many riders prefer practically to ignore their lunch altogether, making a good breakfast and a good meal at night suffice.

After a little experience, the motor-cycle tourist will find himself possessed of an extra sense which will enable him to sense expensive hotels and garages from a glance at the outside thereof. It is surprising how one gets to learn, after a time, how to pick and choose reasonable hotels.

The tourist should obtain a copy of the Raleigh spare parts booklet from The Raleigh Cycle Co., Ltd., Nottingham, in order that he may be sure of the correct price of spare parts should he ever have to obtain these when out of reach of one of the official spare parts stockists given at the end of this book.

Maps. Good maps are useful accessories to a tour, though not an essential, if one intends to keep to main roads. Most of the prettiest scenery in the country lies off the main roads, and a study of the map and local inquiries will often show one how good scenery may be incorporated in the run at the expense of only an extra mile or so.

An excellent series of road maps is issued by the Michelin Tyre Co., which mark all interesting landmarks, spots where good views are obtainable, places of interest worth visiting, and much other useful information to the tourist. Good roads, bad roads, and picturesque ones are all duly marked in a special form.

Touring Abroad. Touring abroad nowadays is made a simple matter, thanks to the action of the road organizations, who will supply members with all necessary information, an oval " G.B." plate and triptiques, which enable the rider to pass from frontier to frontier without depositing customs money at each. Travelling passes are also issued which enable the rider and machine to enter certain countries without undergoing all the formalities which would be otherwise necessary.

CHAPTER IX

MOTOR-CYCLING FOR LADIES

By Marjorie Cottle

THERE are probably still a few persons who object on principle to women motor-cycling ; but, speaking personally and from experience, I would like to assure them that there is really no more health-giving exercise for women who appreciate the benefits of fresh air. Motoring certainly gives one the advantages of fresh air, but unfortunately gives no exercise ; horse-riding, on the other hand, involves rather more bodily exertion than the average woman desires, or requires.

Motor-cycling strikes the happy medium of giving the rider the dual advantage of fresh air and, in my opinion, just the right amount of exercise. But, apart from the point of view of exercise alone, the handiness of the motor-cycle appeals. It can be quickly and easily brought out for little shopping expeditions ; for paying calls, and for the hundred and one little journeys women have to make ; and then, in addition, it will annually be the means of enjoying an ideal holiday.

TECHNICAL KNOWLEDGE

The technical side of a modern motor-cycle need hardly concern the woman rider nowadays. In these days of reliable machines, trouble can be dismissed as an almost negligible quantity. Certainly mechanical knowledge is a useful accomplishment, but it is by no means essential. By far the best means for the would-be rider to acquire the necessary knowledge is to get a male friend to devote an hour or so as teacher. In this way the practical knowledge can be gained with a minimum of trouble, for it is really an extraordinarily simple matter to pick up the rudiments of motor-cycle handling—for a motor-cycle is by no means the complicated machine it looks at first sight, and it is surprising how rapidly one acquires sufficient technical knowledge for ordinary touring.

CLOTHING

In motor-cycling, as in other matters of life, the question of suitable clothing plays an important part. For ordinary short

Fig. 38.—Miss Marjorie Cottle and her 3·48 H.P. Raleigh

spins, such as shopping expeditions, ordinary clothing will well suffice, and a long dust coat or macintosh should be worn. Care, however, must be taken to keep this clear of the chains. For more serious work, such as touring or week-end spins, more suitable clothing should be worn; and, as an example of this, Fig. 38 is an illustration of what I wear, and recommend, whenever out for any considerable ride.

There are one or two pitfalls in connection with this clothing question which should be avoided, and the following information is intended to be of use in guiding the new rider on this very important matter.

By far the most important essential to bear in mind at all times is to keep warm, as far as possible, at all costs; to start with hands and feet warm; and to stop for a few minutes' rest should one get thoroughly cold. It is risky, as well as miserable, to continue riding when thoroughly chilled.

For touring or serious riding, a leather coat is a great boon, if not a necessity; but one should be avoided which has a fur collar. Though this type of coat certainly looks most attractive in fine weather, it gets sodden and uncomfortable in rain and, even in dry weather, the continual chafing of the fur against the neck, combined with the accumulation of dust which fur collects, renders it unsuitable. Therefore, a coat with a plain leather collar is to be preferred, but not with a collar high enough to chafe the face. A very short skirt should be avoided, a tweed skirt of walking length being more suitable; while an old pleated skirt, if of thick material, is still more useful. As an alternative to a skirt, and, generally speaking, preferable, a pair of Bedford cord riding breeches, as men wear, is very comfortable and decidedly more weatherproof than a skirt. In fine weather, woollen stockings and shoes may be worn and, in wet weather, knee-boots or puttees—the former are preferable, since puttees are liable to be too tight and to hamper free circulation, which is, of course, necessary for warmth.

Woollen clothing may be worn next the skin, or, for those who prefer it, silk; but in any case cotton should be avoided, as if the rider has to stop to perform any repairs and get overheated, cotton clothing forms an almost sure way of catching a chill. Silk will be found to be much warmer than wool, and thin silk stockings worn under woollen ones are a great help for winter riding.

Heavy gloves may be worn, or if it is felt that these hamper the control of the machine, thinner gloves may be used in conjunction with handlebar-muffs. Goggles, though they are decidedly ugly things to wear, do certainly protect the eyes, and it is well worth sacrificing a little beauty for the eyes' sake.

Glass goggles should *not* be worn. A pair of celluloid or unsplinterable glass goggles, such as Triplex, are a necessity to a motor-cyclist, and are well worth the extra outlay.

A close-fitting leather hat is a great boon (what is termed a " motoring bonnet " is next to useless) and if possible it should have a brim that can be turned down when riding with the sun in one's eyes. A narrow chin strap is also a great advantage to keep the hat firmly in position, and it need not be conspicuous.

CARE OF THE COMPLEXION

With due care, motor-cycling need not ruin one's skin, if a little forethought is exercised. One fatal mistake should be avoided like a plague, namely, the tendency to smear the face with cream before starting out. This is far from satisfactory, as dust and dirt will collect and work into the skin, defying all efforts when the run is complete to dislodge it. The other alternatives are to run either with a dry skin or with a reasonable coating of powder.

After a day in the wind and sun, if the skin can stand it, washing with rain water is good ; but if not, pure cold cream and a dry towel will usually suffice to remove all dust and dirt. Bathing the eyes in cold water both before and after a run will be found to strengthen them and remove all grit.

ROADSIDE REPAIRS

Trouble will happen, of course, with the best of motor-cycles, though the majority of roadside stops are caused through punctures. Puncture-mending is a messy job at the best of times, and a good tip for keeping dirt out of the nails is to smear them with soap before starting to work. For this purpose, a cake of soap in the pocket is a useful accessory, and has the additional advantage of occasionally coming in useful should the petrol pipe or tank develop a leak; soap will stop up holes effectively. It can be easily removed when the dirty part of the work is over.

If the hands get very dirty or oily, petrol can be used to get it off, but is not to be recommended, as petrol dries up the skin, making it extremely rough. However, if it is absolutely necessary to arrive at the destination with clean hands, petrol may be used, and the smoothness of the skin restored afterwards with glycerine and rose water.

Petrol also forms a first-class medium for removing oil or grease stains from the clothing, but it should be remembered that benzole will not always do for this purpose, as it fades many dyes.

As a final hint for preserving one's freshness on arrival at the destination, a comb and powder-puff form useful accessories for the pocket. On long runs a tooth brush is a useful article to carry.

CHAPTER X

LEGAL HINTS

WHAT to do in case of accidents—Legal matters that affect motor-cyclists.

THE legal necessities, such as licensing and registration, have been fully dealt with in Chapter III. These are items which must be attended to before the machine is taken on the road; and this chapter is more concerned with the matters which affect the motor-cyclist when he is actually out on the road.

In all cases of accidents, or of legal trouble, it is as well to remember that the legal departments of the Automobile Association and other road organizations are always ready to assist members in times of trouble and to give free legal defence in the case of certain road offences.

ACCIDENTS

The most important thing for the rider to know is what to do —or, perhaps more important, what not to do—should he be unfortunate enough to be involved in an accident. The distress of mind which follows any accident occasionally makes a motor-cyclist do many rash things which he should not do, and of which he repents at his leisure. Whatever happens, he should keep his head as far as possible and be alive as much as possible to his own interests. This may seem a selfish principle to uphold, but a very necessary one, as no one but the rider will look after his interests.

The first thing to do is to obtain the names and addresses of two independent witnesses—friendly ones, needless to add. Then, when the inevitable policeman appears, with notebook, remember that civility and a tactful handling of the situation is most likely to foster the greatest justice. (Always remember to call him " officer " by the way, even if he is not one.) See that he takes down the names and addresses of all the parties concerned; notes as to the positions of the vehicles or persons on the road, and a sketch-map, if possible; notes as to warning signs or signals given; the speed at which all were travelling; whether any vehicle was on the wrong side of the road; and any other details which may prove useful should the case ever reach a court. On the rare occasions when no policeman magically appears, the rider should do this himself.

If a person should have been injured by the rider, a doctor

should be called to examine him, so that he can make an independent report of his condition.

Name and Address. To anyone who complains that the motorist has committed an offence of driving to the common danger, the driver must give his name and address. The penalty for refusing, or for giving a false name and address, is £20, with heavier penalties for subsequent offences. He may be arrested without warrant by a constable who saw the alleged offence committed, whether the constable is in uniform or not. The owner, if required, must give all the information in his power which may lead to the identification of the driver and, if he does not do so, is himself liable to the same penalty as the driver.

In the case of an accident, as already stated, the names and addresses of all concerned, and of witnesses, should be obtained. On the other hand, if the rider is asked to give his name and address, he should certainly do so, as refusal would go heavily against him in a court.

Do not engage in correspondence without legal advice or, if this is not taken, make it clear in all letters that they are written without prejudice to your legal rights; and refrain from making statements, either at the time of the accident or afterwards, which may afterwards be construed into an admission of liability.

On no account offer money to an injured party, for motives of sympathy may be misconstrued into an admission of legal liability.

The Order to Stop. A person in charge of a horse may order a motor-cyclist to stop; so may a constable in uniform or a person injured by the machine. In other cases, when requested to stop, it may be best to take no notice, unless it is a case of an accident, or someone in trouble.

Insurance. In cases of damage to the machine, the insurance company should be notified as soon as possible. The general rule of insurance companies is that they must be notified within three days. A letter giving formal notice of a claim should be sent, when the company will send, in reply, a large form to be filled up.

Endorsement of Licence. All convictions under the Motor Car Act, 1903, may be endorsed on the back of the licence, except a conviction for obstruction, and the first and second conviction for exceeding the speed limit. The holder of a licence which has been endorsed may, upon renewal, or at any time on payment of 5s., have a new licence free from endorsements if he has not during a period of at least three years had any conviction endorsed.

LEGAL HINTS

Staying Proceedings. For certain minor offences, such as using a motor cycle with an expired licence, a Council may sometimes, under the Roads Act, 1920, write to the offender that they will stay proceedings if the offender will pay a certain sum, which is usually the equivalent of what the fine would be. If the offender knows that he is in the wrong, it is usually best to fall in with this arrangement and so save the cost of defence at court ; on the other hand, if the offender is reasonably sure of winning his case, he can afford to go to court with it.

Furious Driving. A person driving furiously renders himself liable to conviction for the following offences, under the Highway Acts.
1. Driving to the common danger.
2. Exceeding the speed limit.
3. If anyone injured, indictment for causing bodily harm.
4. If anyone killed, indictment for manslaughter.
5. To arrest by any person, whether constable or not, who sees the offence committed, under the Highway Acts.

Arrest. The driver is liable to arrest by a police-constable (whether in uniform or not) if he refuses his name and address, refuses to produce his licence on demand, or if his machine does not bear the identification (registration) mark.

Number Plates. The numbers on the plates must be of the dimensions given in Chapter III, and the plate must be properly fixed and not in any way obscured or rendered not easily distinguishable, or not properly illuminated at night. Either the front or rear plate may be illuminated. Pillion riders should take care that dresses do not overlap the rear number-plate, —unlikely, nowadays, but still just possible.

Warning of Approach. It is compulsory to give audible warning of approach, where necessary, by means of a horn, bell, or other suitable instrument.

Exhaust Cut-out. It is illegal to use an exhaust cut-out or any device which enables the exhaust gases to escape without first passing through the silencer.

Reverse Gear. When a motor cycle weighs more than 7 cwt. unladen, a reverse gear must be fitted. As, however, the heaviest of the standard Raleigh combinations does not approach this, this regulation need not worry the Raleigh owner.

Registration Book. The registration book should be kept in a safe place at home and not on the machine. The book must be sent to the County Council when any change is made to the machine, such as when a sidecar is added to the machine, or any alteration made in horse-power or other detail entered in the registration book.

The book must also be sent to the County Council should the machine be sold or its ownership changed, or on its being broken up, destroyed, or permanently sent out of the United Kingdom.

Obstruction. The machine must not be left for an unreasonable or unnecessary time on the highway so as to cause an obstruction. In many towns a machine may not be left in certain streets and, in these cases, inquiry of the nearest police officer will discover the location of the nearest parking-place. In many towns the A.A. has arranged parking-places, which are distinguished by A.A. signs.

Time Limit for Summons. Unless warned at the time the offence is committed notice of an intended prosecution for exceeding the speed limit must be given to the driver or owner of the vehicle within twenty-one days of the alleged offence.

Right of Appeal. A person convicted of any offence under the Motor Car Act, 1903, has the right of appeal to the next Court of Quarter Sessions, provided he did not plead "guilty," in courts other than Metropolitan. A right of appeal lies against an order disqualifying any person from obtaining a driver's licence.

Speed Limit. Many riders believe that the speed limit has been abolished, but, at the present, at any rate, this is not so ; and, according to the strict letter of the law, no vehicle may be driven at a speed exceeding 20 miles per hour on the highway. Special limits of 8 or 10 miles per hour are fixed in certain towns and villages. These must be strictly observed.

Police Traps. To ensure the observance of the speed limit, it has been the custom of the police to time the passage of motor traffic over a measured stretch of road—usually 100 yds. Formerly the practice was to choose an open stretch for this, where motor-cyclists would go "all-out." ; but nowadays the tendency is more to time them in places where their high speed really constitutes a danger.

Danger Signs. Fig. 39 shows the danger signs employed on the roads. The Automobile Association has also put up, for the benefit of its members, signs warning them of dangerous corners, schools, fords. etc., and signs giving names of villages

LEGAL HINTS

and distances from the nearest towns. The R.A.C. danger sign, rarely met with, should always be well heeded, as there is invariably real danger where they are placed. The C.T.C. and N.C.U. danger signs are also exceedingly useful to the motor-cyclist.

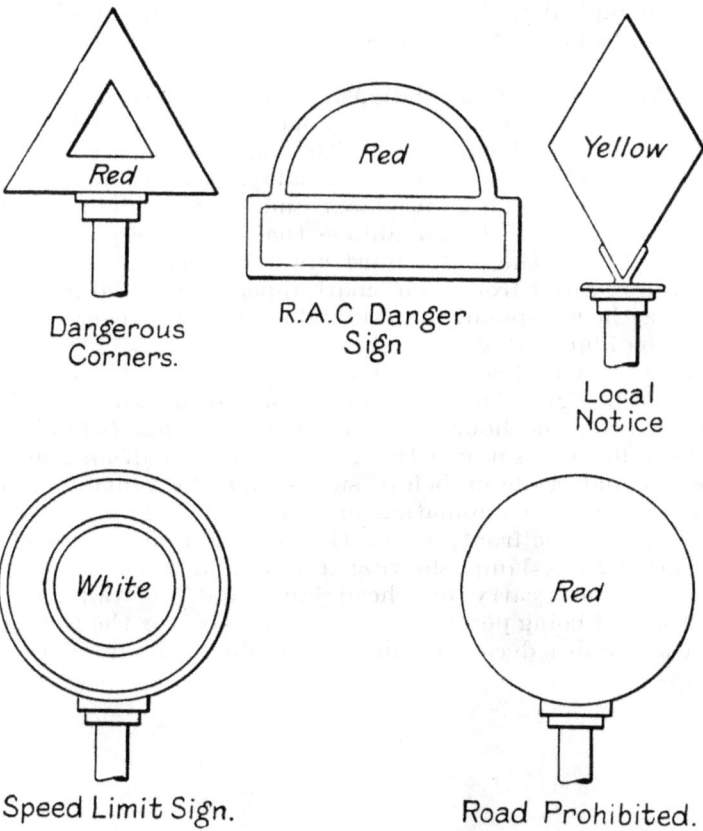

FIG. 39.—CONVENTIONAL ROAD SIGNS

There is a growing tendency nowadays for owners of houses with drives to put up private requests for passing drivers to slow up; in some districts these preponderate to an annoying extent, but, generally speaking, they form a useful guide to the motor-cyclist to points where he should look for vehicles coming out into the road.

Leaving the Machine. A motor-cycle may not be left unattended with the engine running, however short the period.

Storing Petrol. Up to 60 gallons of petrol may be kept stored for private use if it is kept in 2-gallon tins marked "Petroleum Spirit—highly inflammable," so long as it is at least 20 ft. from any building or other inflammable goods. If this condition cannot be complied with, a special licence must be obtained, at a small fee, from the local licensing authority.

The New Lighting Regulations. Every modern motor-cycle is equipped with two number plates, one at the rear, and one at the front in line with the machine. The numbers must be painted or transferred on to these plates. Nowadays several concerns market very smart cast aluminium plates, and certain riders may prefer these. They have the advantage that they are easier to keep clean, and since the plates must always be legible, this is a feature which, apart from their smart appearance, is largely responsible for their popularity. At night time the rear plate must always be illuminated.

Under the new Road Transport (Lighting) Act, which came into effect on the 22nd April, 1928, the hours of darkness are defined as being from one hour after sunset to one hour before sunrise, during official "summer-time," and from half-an-hour after sunset to half-an-hour before sunrise for the remainder of the year. A sidecar combination must carry two lamps showing a white light to the front, one on the cycle and one on the sidecar, together with a lamp showing a red light to the rear. Solo machines must carry one head lamp and one tail lamp, red reflectors not being permitted. It is necessary for the tail lamp of either a solo or sidecar machine to illuminate the number plate.

CHAPTER XI

ON BUYING AND SELLING AN OLD MACHINE

BUYING A SECOND-HAND MACHINE

For financial reasons, the reader may contemplate buying a second-hand machine in preference to a new one, or he may want to do so in order to have an old machine to learn on instead of risking damage to a brand new motor-cycle. In either case, for the novice, there is as much risk in buying a second-hand motor-cycle as in buying a horse, and the inexperienced purchaser should always take an expert friend with him to examine the machine before making a final decision.

Make and Year. Competition is so strong in the motor-cycle market that artificial inflation of prices is practically unknown; and, where a new machine is concerned, the purchaser gets value corresponding to the amount he pays. But, in the case of second-hand motor-cycles, the seller may be asking a price out of all proportion to the value of the machine he offers, and it is therefore advisable to obtain some idea of the current prices of whatever make of machine the reader has in view.

The importance of buying only a machine with a well-known name and reputation cannot be over-emphasized; not only does this ensure the reliability of the machine, but enables the rider being sure of being able to obtain spare parts subsequently, should occasion arise. Study of the columns of second-hand motor-cycles advertised for sale weekly in the motor-cycle papers will give the prospective purchaser a very valuable guide to current prices asked for second-hand mounts of the particular make he fancies.

The year of make of the machine should be ascertained from the owner's registration book, as a skilful "shark" may easily transform an antediluvian piece of machinery to bear a passing resemblance to a fairly recent machine.

Examining the Machine. The frame should be carefully examined for cracks, side-play, and loose joints. The condition of the tyres (and if there is time and opportunity, the state of the inner tubes), the wheel bearings, the condition of the tools and accessories, the head and front forks, should all be carefully examined. If a sidecar is fitted, the method and state of its attachment should be noted. Then if the purchaser is satisfied with the general condition of the machine, the engine should be subjected to a careful examination.

Testing the Engine. The engine should be turned over by means of the kick-starter to ascertain that the compression is good. Then it should be rotated, and any noise or signs of wear noted. If there is much wear, it will probably be most apparent in the valves and valve gear, but these parts are easily and cheaply replaced. If the valves have been repeatedly ground in, this fact will be apparent, for the valve seats will be relatively wide and deeply sunk, as shown in Fig. 27. This is a sign either of careless usage or of old age, and should be duly considered. The valve gear mechanism should be exposed and examined; if the wheels and cams are worn, they will require renewal.

The condition of the piston and cylinder cannot be easily ascertained from a superficial examination; but if there is any indication of the piston loosely fitting and slapping in its cylinder, it will usually show that the cylinder has worn oval in shape: in this case, it will need re-grinding and an oversize piston fitted. An alloy piston is loosely fitting when cold, and this must not be mistaken for the bad fitting of a cast-iron piston in its cylinder.

Trial Run. If the machine gives reasonable satisfaction from the above superficial examination, the purchaser should insist on a trial run, so that he may be satisfied with the control and general running. In the case of a combination, the owner may ride in the sidecar, to prevent loss; but in the case of a solo machine, the owner might quite reasonably demand a deposit as a token of good faith before allowing the trial run. But, in any case, the trial run is a most important part of the transaction, as by no other means can the capabilities of the machine be judged. It should be run at speed and slowly in top gear, and taken up the nearest local approach to a test hill and its performances carefully noted.

Stolen Property. The reader is advised to make quite sure that the seller is the real owner of the machine, for if he purchases and the machine is subsequently claimed by the rightful owner, he must return the machine to the real owner, and has no redress except the doubtful one of suing the vendor—who will have probably disappeared in the meantime. Examination of the registration book will show the name and address of the owner, and comparison of signatures on any letters that may

BUYING AND SELLING OLD MACHINES

have passed and that on the registration book will help to show whether the vendor is the genuine owner.

The Deposit System. If the machine is purchased through the trade paper advertisements of second-hand machines, it is usually possible for the vendor to deposit his purchase money with the editor of the paper concerned. Then when the purchaser is satisfied with the machine and agrees to purchase it, the paper hands over the money to the vendor. This system is useful where the machine is sold to a purchaser who cannot come personally to test the machine.

SELLING A SECOND-HAND MACHINE

The foregoing information indicates in some degree the question a purchaser is likely to ask, and before selling the machine it should be placed in reasonable selling condition. If this is done, a higher price is commanded, correspondence and complaints after the sale is completed are avoided, and it saves making excuses when the prospective purchaser points out the defects.

Selling Through an Agency. Several firms undertake to sell second-hand machines, the usual procedure being to value the machine and to allow the agent a commission on that price. Such agents usually sell the machine at a higher price than the owner would obtain privately, so that it is usually well worth while to adopt this method, so long as only a reliable firm is dealt with.

Selling by Advertising. This is an excellent method of selling, because the trade papers classify the machines. so that the man wishing to purchase a Raleigh has only to look down the small advertisement columns of one of the motor-cycle papers to compare prices. The fact cannot be ignored that a prospective purchaser of a second-hand machine probably looks at one of these papers, and therefore this method is to be highly recommended.

Money can be more easily wasted in advertising than in any other form of money-spending, so that the seller should carefully consider the features of his machine before writing out his advertisement. If price is the feature, put it boldly at the beginning of the advertisement, so that the figure stands out. As the first word of these advertisements usually appears in capital letters, the choice of this word is important. For instance, the word " Raleigh " should not be placed first, as one does not want to emphasize the word " Raleigh " in a column advertising entirely Raleigh machines. If the machine is one of this year's models, the word " 1930 " can well be placed first ; if the price is really attractive, place it first.

The seller's genuine name and address is usually better than a box number in obtaining replies, as purchasers are often, though needlessly, suspicious of the latter. The season of the year should be considered ; a better price is obtained in the spring than in, say, the month before the annual Cycle Show at Olympia. If the tax has been paid, make a point of this in the advertisement.

Registration Formalities. The rules relating to the registration book when the machine changes hands should be carefully complied with. Full details of the procedure are given in the book, and they should be carefully carried out. And, finally, if the purchaser pays by cheque, get it cleared before parting with the machine, unless he is known personally as reliable.

CHAPTER XII

USEFUL INFORMATION

TABLE OF GRADIENTS

Gradient	Per Cent	No. of Feet Rise or Fall in 1 Mile
1 in 2	50	2640
1 ,, 2½	40	2112
1 ,, 3	34	1760
1 ,, 3½	28	1508
1 ,, 4	25	1320
1 ,, 5	20	1056
1 ,, 6	17	880
1 ,, 7	14	754
1 ,, 8	12½	660
1 ,, 9	11	587
1 ,, 10	10	528
1 ,, 11	9	480
1 ,, 12	8	440
1 ,, 13	7¾	406
1 ,, 14	7	377
1 ,, 15	6½	352
1 ,, 16	6¼	330
1 ,, 17	6	311
1 ,, 18	5½	293
1 ,, 19	5	278
1 ,, 20	5	264
1 ,, 25	4	211
1 ,, 30	3·3	176
1 ,, 35	2·8	154
1 ,, 40	2½	132

EQUIVALENT SPEEDS

Speeds in m.p.h.	Time Taken to Cover 1 Mile.
10	6 minutes
15	4 ,,
20	3 ,,
25	2 ,, 24 seconds
30	2 ,,
35	1 ,, 42$\frac{6}{7}$,,
40	1 ,, 30 ,,
50	1 ,, 12 ,,
60	1 ,,

FORMULA FOR APPROXIMATE ENGINE REVOLUTIONS

To ascertain number of engine revolutions per minute—

m.p.h. × gear × 13 = r.p.m.

For instance, supposing an O.H.V. Raleigh sports model reaches 70 m.p.h., the number of engine revolutions per minute can be ascertained by multiplying the speed by the gear and by 13. Thus,

$$70 \times 5 \cdot 5 \times 13$$
$$= 381 \times 13$$
$$= 5005 \text{ r.p.m}$$

This formula is accurate enough for all ordinary purposes of the general rider.

FORMULAE FOR H.P.

S = stroke in centimetres
D = diameter of cylinder in centimetres
R = revolutions per minute
N = number of cylinders

R.A.C. Formula, H.P. $= \dfrac{D^2 \times N}{16 \cdot 13}$

A.C.U. Formula, H.P. = 100 c.c. equals 1 h.p.

These two formulae are reckoned as the horse-power when the engine is running at 2000 r.p.m.

A more accurate formula is the Dendy Marshall, which is

$$\text{H.P.} = \dfrac{D^2 \times S \times N \times R}{200{,}000}$$

Thus, according to the three formulae, the horse-power of the 3·48 h.p. Raleigh engine, which has a bore of 71 mm. and a stroke of 88 mm., giving a c.c. of 348, is as follows—

R.A.C. $\quad \dfrac{7 \cdot 1^2 \times 1}{16 \cdot 13} = \dfrac{50 \cdot 41}{16 \cdot 13} = 3 \cdot 125$ h.p.

A.C.U. $\quad$ 348 c.c. = 3·48 h.p.

Dendy Marshall. $\dfrac{50 \cdot 41 \times 8 \cdot 8 \times 1 \times 2000}{200{,}000} = \dfrac{887{,}216}{200{,}000} = 4 \cdot 43608$ h.p.

TYRE SIZE EQUIVALENTS

65 millimetres	=	2½ in.	105 millimetres	=	4¼ in.
80 ,,	=	3 ,,	600 ,,	=	24 ,,
85 ,,	=	3¼ ,,	650 ,,	=	26 ,,
90 ,,	=	3½ ,,	700 ,,	=	28 ,,
100 ,,	=	4 ,,	750 ,,	=	30 ,,

LIGHTING-UP TIME TABLE

(Greenwich Mean Time)

Add 1 hour during Summer time period

January

1	4.30 p.m.	18	4.52 p.m.
4	4.33 ,,	22	4.59 ,,
8	4.38 ,,	25	5. 4 ,,
12	4.42 ,,	29	5.11 ,,
15	4.48 ,,		

February

2	5.17 p.m.	15	5.44 p.m.
5	5.26 ,,	19	5.52 ,,
8	5.31 ,,	22	5.57 ,,
12	5.39 ,,	26	6. 3 ,,

March

1	6. 8 p.m.	18	6.37 p.m.
4	6.13 ,,	22	6.44 ,,
8	6.20 ,,	25	4.49 ,,
11	6.25 ,,	29	6.55 ,,
15	6.32 ,,		

April

1	7. 1 p.m.	19	7.32 p.m.
5	7. 7 ,,	22	7.36 ,,
8	7.12 ,,	26	7.42 ,,
12	7.19 ,,	29	7.47 ,,
15	7.24 ,,		

May

3	7.53 p.m.	20	8.20 p.m.
6	7.58 ,,	24	8.25 ,,
10	8. 5 ,,	27	8.29 ,,
13	8. 9 ,,	31	8.34 ,,
17	8.15 ,,		

June

3	8.37 p.m.	17	8.47 p.m.
7	8.40 ,,	21	8.48 ,,
10	8.43 ,,	24	8.49 ,,
14	8.45 ,,	28	8.49 ,,

July

1	8.48 p.m.	19	8.35 p.m.
5	8.47 ,,	22	8.31 ,,
8	8.45 ,,	26	8.27 ,,
12	8.42 ,,	29	8.22 ,,
15	8.40 ,,		

August

2	8.45 p.m.	19	7.43 p.m.
5	8.10 ,,	23	7.35 ,,
9	8. 3 ,,	26	7.29 ,,
12	7.57 ,,	30	7.20 ,,
16	7.49 ,,		

September

2	7.14 p.m.	16	6.42 p.m.
6	7. 5 ,,	20	6.33 ,,
9	6.58 ,,	23	6.26 ,,
13	6.49 ,,	27	6.17 ,,

October

2	6. 5 p.m.	18	5.30 p.m.
4	6. 1 ,,	21	5.23 ,,
7	5.54 ,,	25	5.15 ,,
11	5.45 ,,	28	5.10 ,,
14	5.38 ,,		

November

1	5. 2 p.m.	18	4.35 p.m.
4	4.57 ,,	22	4.31 ,,
8	4.50 ,,	25	4.27 ,,
11	4.45 ,,	29	4.24 ,,
15	4.39 ,,		

December

2	4 22 p.m.	20	4.21 p.m.
6	4.20 ,,	23	4.22 ,,
9	4.19 ,,	27	4.25 ,,
13	4.19 ,,	30	4.28 ,,
16	4.20 ,,		

RALEIGH MOTOR-CYCLE SPARE PARTS STOCKISTS

ENGLAND

BEDFORDSHIRE—

Bedford	Arthur Gell	6a St. Loyes
Luton	H. G. Partridge & Co.	Chapel Street

BERKSHIRE—

Newbury	A. C. Bishop, Ltd.	135–136 Bartholomew Street
Reading	H. Julian	84 Broad Street
Wallingford	F. H. Jenkins	7 Market Place
Wantage	Wantage Motor Co.	Mill Street
Windsor	J. Taylor	Oxford Road
Wokingham	Perkins Bros.	40 Broad Street

BUCKINGHAMSHIRE—

Beaconsfield	F. Ellis	High Street
Slough	A. E. Mann	81 High Street
Stoke Poges	B. Burgess	

CAMBRIDGESHIRE—

Cambridge	G. & J. Dawson	60 Regent Street

CHESHIRE—

Altrincham	W. Richardson	8–10 Oxford Road
Birkenhead	R. Edmunds	9 Whetstone Lane
Chester	Marstons (Chester), Ltd.	Bridge Street
Crewe	F. Wooldridge & Sons	High Street
Macclesfield	T. Simister	24 Jordangate
New Brighton	Apperley Bros.	Pickering Road
Northwich	Thompson & Sons	Castle Street
Rockferry	Hesketh Bros.	471 New Chester Street
Sandbach	G. Wakefield	High Street Garage

CORNWALL—

Bodmin	W. H. Jane & Sons	
Bude	Cann, Medland & Co.	The Garage
Camborne	C. H. Penny	71 Trelowarren Street
Helston	Mrs. R. Lory	16 Wendron Street
Launceston	S. Sluggett	Exeter Street
Newquay	Hawkey & Cocking	Fore Street
Penzance	Taylor's Garage, Ltd.	Greenmarket
Redruth	Mrs. C. E. Berryman	Redruth Garage
St. Austell	W. J. Comley	

CUMBERLAND—

Brampton	R. J. Nixon	Front Street
Carlisle	W. T. Tiffen	Caldew Bridge
Egremont	H. Lewthwaite	1a Main Street
Flimby	R. G. Baxter	
Longtown	Longtown Motor Depot	Bridge Street

DERBYSHIRE—

Ashbourne	Kennedy & Co.	Market Place
Belper	Day's Garage	King Street

DERBYSHIRE—(contd.)

Chesterfield	M. Brooks	Holywell Street
Clowne	Ernest Sherwin	35 North Road
Draycott	Oxford Cycle Co., Ltd.	Victoria Road
Matlock	Stanley Fearn	Bakewell Road
Melbourne	H. Wall	Market Place
Woodseats	W. Williams	783 Chesterfield Road

DEVONSHIRE—

Axminster	Axminster Garage Co.	Lyme Street
Barnstaple	Arch. Jones	High Street
Exeter	Wippell Bros. & Row	243–244 High Street
,,	P. Pike & Co., Ltd.	Alphington Street
Honiton	Moor's Garage	
Kingsbridge	L. Bowman	102 Fore Street
Plymouth	P. Pike & Co., Ltd.	Union Street
Teignmouth	H. Williams & Co.	16 Bitton Street
Tiverton	Batten & Thorne, Ltd.	Gold Street

DORSET

Dorchester	Tilley's	South Street
Weymouth	Tilley's	The Esplanade

DURHAM—

Barnard Castle	E. Watson	20 Galgate
Bishop Auckland	H. Richardson	145 Newgate Street
Chester-le-Street	E. W. Maughan	61 Front Street
Crook	Gill Bros.	23 Hope Street
Darlington	The Duplex Motor Co.	Grange Road
Durham	G. L. Gibson	23 North Road
Fencehouses	E. J. Smith	16 Morton Crescent
Ferryhill	Jones Bros.	Darlington Road
Gateshead	O. Carmichael	81–83 High West Street
Stanhope	J. Walton	Front Street
Stockton-on-Tees	Stan. Jones	Green Dragon Garage, Finkle Street
Sunderland	Dunn & Jameson	100–106 Hylton Road

ESSEX—

Braintree	George Cox	Payne Road
Chadwell Heath	Sissley's Motor Supply Co.	The Pavement
Chelmsford	J. Day	Market Buildings
Colchester	W. Paull & Co.	6, 8, 10 Barrack Street
East Ham	Lovetts, Ltd.	439 Barking Road
Epping	Cottis & Son	High Street
Forest Gate	Lovett's, Ltd.	418 Romford Road
,,	L. J. & Co.	24 Woodford Road, E.7
Romford	The Rhosha Motor Co.	Bank Mews Works, South St.
Southend	W. Tickett & Sons	33 Queen's Road
Stanford-le-Hope	F. G. Stacey	Southend Road Garage

GLOUCESTERSHIRE—

Bristol	H. Haskins & Sons	14 City Road
Cheltenham	Cheltenham Motor & Cycle Co.	82 High Street

SPARE PARTS STOCKISTS 107

GLOUCESTERSHIRE—(contd.)
Gloucester	T. G. Hall	25–27 Barton Street
Lydney	Watts Factors, Ltd.	
Stroud	Wicliffe Motor Co.	Russell Street

HAMPSHIRE—
Aldershot	Phillips Bros.	Birchett Road
Bournemouth	P. W. Surplice	Poole Hill
Farnborough	F. Coney	Victoria Road
Hartley Wintney	H. Cook	High Street
Overton	H. J. Gifford	
Petersfield	Tew & Son	Lavant Street
Portsmouth	Suitalls	258 Commercial Road
Southampton	The Birmingham and Coventry Cycle Co.	149–151 Above Bar
Winchester	Winchester Cycle and Motor Co.	Jewry Street

HEREFORDSHIRE—
Hereford	E. B. Howell	14 and 15 Commercial Road
,,	The Hereford Motor Co.	City Garage

HERTFORDSHIRE—
Hitchin	J. Chalkley & Son	Brand Street
King's Langley	E. H. MacMillan	High Street
Letchworth	Mason's Garage	Eastcheap
Royston	A. Pepper, Reenes and Haywood	Melbourn Street
St. Albans	Clarkes	London Road
Watford	G. Jones & Son	Market Street

HUNTINGDONSHIRE—
Huntingdon	Murkett Bros.	St. Mary's Works

KENT—
Ashford	The Ashford Motor and Engineering Co.	Middle Street
Bexley Heath	Martin & Son	Broadway
Bromley	J. L. Love & Co.	21 Park Road
Canterbury	G. R. Barrett & Son	30 St. Peter's Street
Catford	F. Parks & Son	10 Sangley Road
Gravesend	The Service Garage, Ltd.	119–125 Wrotham Road
Herne Bay	Curling & Lukehurst, Ltd.	King's Road Garage
Lee	T. J. Ross	86 High Street
Maidstone	Mockford & Smith	Tonbridge Road
Margate	Kerr's Garage	Northdown Road, Cliftonville
Ramsgate	A and B Garages, Ltd.	Grange Road
Rochester	Rootes, Ltd.	The Motor House
Tunbridge Wells	Read Bros.	4 and 6 Goods Station Road
Whitstable	Haywood & Ashcroft	43 Canterbury Road

LANCASHIRE—
Blackburn	Slater's	3 Lord Street
Bolton	Madgwick & Co.	79 Knowsley Street
Burnley	R. Pollard	Mitre Works, Padiham Rd.
Bury	Thomas Dobson	4 Elton Road

LANCASHIRE—(contd.)

Clitheroe	J. & F. Bentham	Market Place
Goosnargh	Charles Fletcher	Crompton's Garage
Great Crosby	L. Myerscough	25 Liverpool Road
Leigh	F. Timms & Co., Ltd.	Leigh Road
Liverpool	The Colmore Depot	Paradise Street
,,	Victor Horsman, Ltd.	7 Mount Pleasant
,,	J. Roberts & Son	182 Walton Breck Road, Anfield
Longsight	C. R. Cowan	560–566 Stockport Road
Manchester	Tom Davies	229 Deansgate
Northenden	G. F. Swinglehurst	71 Palatine Road
Oldham	H. Fenwick	65 Mumps
Preston	Marks & Baron, Ltd.	215–217 Lancaster Road
Rochdale	A. E. Stott	393 Manchester Rd., Sudden
St. Helen's	W. Cook	107 Church Street
Southport	Seal & Ball	25 London Street
Warrington	F. A. Crabtree	Bridge Foot
,,	J. Danks	3 Bewsey Street

LEICESTERSHIRE—

Leicester	W. E. Pym & Co.	Belgrave Gate

LINCOLNSHIRE—

Boston	F. Launchbury	5, 7, and 14 Dolphin Lane
Donington	G. Dawson & Sons	High Street
Grimsby	Jas. Plastow & Son	13, 15, and 19 Osborne St.
Lincoln	West's (Lincoln), Ltd.	115c and 115d High Street
Wellingore	C. B. Aram	
Wragby	Dove & Son	Market Place

LONDON—

London	Godfrey's, Ltd.	208 Great Portland St., W.1., and 232 Stamford Hill, N.16
,,	R. G. Houchin, Ltd.	188 High Street, Peckham, S.E.15
,,	Berry's	391 Commercial Road, Stepney
,,	The Putney Bridge Garage	222 Putney Bridge Road, Putney, S.W.
,,	The Service Co. (London) Ltd.	273–274 High Holborn, W.C.1
,,	The Service or Spares Depot	7 Seymour Place, Marble Arch
,,	Turner Bros.	29 Green Lanes, N.13
,,	Turner's Stores	181 Railway Approach, Shepherd's Bush
Greenwich	Sam. E. Clapham	27 Stockwell Road, S.E.10
Lee	T. J. Ross	86 High Road, S.E.13
Woolwich	Cleare & Co.	125 High Street, S.E.18

MIDDLESEX—

Acton	George Clarke (Motors), Ltd.	275 High Street
Ealing	Kay's	Bond Street
Hendon	E. J. Rogers	42 Church Road
Wood Green	Lamb's, Ltd.	50 High Road

SPARE PARTS STOCKISTS

NORFOLK—

Fakenham	Southgate's, Ltd.	Oak Street
Harleston	Johnstone's Wavney Works	
King's Lynn	King's Lynn Motors, Ltd.	London Road
New Buckenham	Fox Bros.	
Norwich	H. Chapman	42 Duke Street
Thetford	W. & G. Lambert, Ltd.	Castle Street

NORTHAMPTONSHIRE—

Desborough	F. Burditt	Station Road
Kettering	J. Kemp	Rockingham Road
Northampton	Chas. Ashby	Clare Street and Spencer Road
Peterborough	G. L. Julyan	48 Cowgate
Wellingborough	H. V. Briggs	High Street and Church St.

NORTHUMBERLAND—

Bedlington	Wm. Elliott	West End Garage
Blyth	A. S. Mole & Son	11 Havelock Street
Hexham	Forster & Low, Ltd.	Hencotes' Garage
Lowick	L. Robinson	Beal Station Motor Works
Morpeth	Ralph Main	45 Newgate Street
Newcastle-on-Tyne	The Dene Motor Co.	Haymarket
Whitley Bay	H. Schofield	57 Victoria Terrace

NOTTINGHAMSHIRE—

Beeston	R. S. Cudlip & Co.	Woollaton Road Garage
Bulwell	Robinson Bros.	Highbury Road
Creswell	Willis Jones	Mansfield Road
Mansfield	Wm. Bull	46 Westgate
Newark	C. E. Ford & Son	Cycle and Motor Depot
Nottingham	H. Edgson	Ilkeston Road
,,	D. H. Mosley	City Buildings, Carrington Street
,,	Harold Petty (Nottm.), Ltd.	Shakespeare Street
,,	A. S. Gibbons	56 Peverill Street
Ruddington	R. Grice	Midland Railway
Selston	J. S. Wilde	Nottingham Road
Sutton-in-Ashfield	E. Hutchinson	Market Place
Worksop	Campion Depot	Bridge Street

OXFORDSHIRE—

Banbury	George L. Ginger	17 and 18 Parson's Street
Forest Hill (Nr. Oxford)	W. Turner	
Oxford	The Layton Garages	30 Holywell Street

SHROPSHIRE—

Market Drayton	Halloway Bros.	Cheshire Street
Oswestry	E. J. Gittins, Ltd.	35 Church Street
Shrewsbury	J. C. Pickering	49 Mardel
Whitchurch	W. H. Smith & Co. (Whitchurch), Ltd.	

SOMERSETSHIRE—

Bath	F. C. Wallace	Fountain Buildings
Kingsbury Episcopi	J. C. Bishop	
Minehead	Bradbeer Bros.	Friday Street

SOMERSETSHIRE—(contd.)
Taunton	A. C. Westlake	49 Station Road
Yeovil	James Moffat	Opposite Town Hall

STAFFORDSHIRE—
Burslem	J. Alcock	Market Place
Burton-on-Trent	Gilbert, Field & Co.	Station Street
Kingsley	T. R. Smith	Kingsley Motor Garage
Leek	Leek Cycle Co.	Haywood Street
Longton	Leese's Garage	Meir Lane
Meir	Leese's Garage	49 Meir Lane
Stafford	S. E. Adderley	Marston Road Garage
Stoke	Nicholson Bros.	Wolfe Street
Stone	Attwood & Co.	High Street
Tittensor	W. Abbotts	Berne House
Wolverhampton	Cyril Williams	Chapel Ash

SUFFOLK—
Bury St. Edmunds	E. F. Scott & Son	6 Brentqoval Street
Eye	F. E. Whant & Son	Broad Street
Felixstowe	Hinsley & Hutley	Hamilton Road
Lowestoft	Taylor Bros.	75 London Road North
Stowmarket	Stannard & Co.	Tavern Street

SURREY—
Frensham	Heath Bros.	
Guildford	J. E. Jackson	1 Portsmouth Road
Reigate	Finch & Sons	Bell Street
Sutton	J. Robins	2 and 3 Carshalton Road
Weybridge	Bowman & Sons	Baker Street
Woking	Godwin Bros.	85 Chertsey Road

SUSSEX—
Arundel	Martin's Garage	Tarrant Street
Bexhill	T. E. Marchant	52 St. Leonard's Road
Crawley	C. Gadsdon	5 Brighton Road
Eastbourne	Bradshaw's	10 Terminus Road
Horsham	Jackson Bros.	65–67 London Road
Hove	Bradshaw's	6 Western Road
Lewes	Arthur E. Rugg	1–3 Fisher Street
Midhurst	Victor Dale	North Street
Pulborough	Gray & Rowsall	Bury Gate
Robertsbridge	T. Croft	12 Station Road
St. Leonards-on-Sea	W. T. Charles	The Junction Garage, Silverhill
Uckfield	G. Cyster	Bodlett's Garage

WARWICKSHIRE—
Birmingham	The Premier Motor Co.	Aston Road
Coventry	S. H. Newsome & Co., Ltd.	6 Hales Street
Four Oaks	C. Brander	Mere Green
Leamington Spa	G. Main & Co.	6 Bedford Street
Nuneaton	J. G. Collins	9–11 Riversley Road
Rugby	G. T. Hilton & Co.	North Street
Stratford-on-Avon	S. Duffill	Wren's Nest Garage
Warwick	D. Hackleton	1 St. John's
Wolvey (Nr. Hinckley)	R. White	Service Garage

SPARE PARTS STOCKISTS

WESTMORLAND—

Holme	Ed. Taylor	Milnthorpe Road
Kirkby Lonsdale	J. Coultert	Main Street
Windermere	R. Smith	The Garage

WILTSHIRE—

Devizes	F. W. Way	46 New Park Street
Salisbury	Woodrow & Co. (Salisbury), Ltd.	5–7 Castle Street
Swindon	Hutton's	Devizes Road
Trowbridge	W. B. Stephens	Castle Cycle Works
Warminster	A. J. Dale	7 Silver Street

WORCESTERSHIRE—

Bromsgrove	W. H. Chapman	High Street
Kidderminster	J. Sanders	58 New Road
Stourbridge	Pearson's Cycle Depot	Market Street

YORKSHIRE : East Riding—

Bridlington	Austin & Doran	Quay Road
Hessle	Hessle Motor Co.	Market Place
Hull	Jordan & Co.	93 Prospect Street
Richmond	Rodber & Sons	Market Place
Norton	C. Bower	Motor Exchange, Church Street
York	J. D. Shearsmith	Blossom Street

YORKSHIRE : North Riding—

Kirbymoorside	W. Hodgson	West End Garage
Middlesbrough	Pallister, Yare & Cobb	St. John's Garage, Marton Road
Slingsby	T. E. Dosser & Sons	
Scarborough	J. S. Atkinson	103 Falsgrave Road

YORKSHIRE : West Riding—

Askern	E. Claybourn	The Garage
Barnsley	F. Caffrey	10–12 Doncaster Road
Bradford	Denham & Bottomley	220 Manningham Lane
Castleford	Sydney Batten & Sons	Carlton Street
Cudworth	J. Moore	Palace Cycle Stores
Dinnington	H. M. Barlow	68 Laughton Road
Doncaster	W. E. Clark & Co.	Station Road
Gargrave	W. Gill & Sons	
Halifax	The Halifax Motor Exchange	25 Horton Street
Harrogate	P. Calvert	Cheltenham Parade
Hoyland	G. Neil	Aero Garage
Huddersfield	The One-Tree Motor Co.	Oxford Street
Knaresborough	Thos. Clapham	High Street
Keighley	A. Shuttleworth & Co.	121 Skipton Road
Leeds	Henry Smith	119 View Lane
Maltby	A. & H. Brown	The Garage
Normanton	W. B. Motor & Engineering Co.	Church Lane
Penistone	J. Penn & Co.	Bridge End
Pontefract	S. Batten & Sons	Bridge Street
Rotherham	E. Cross	Effingham Square
Sheffield	M. Brooks	Moorhead
Skipton	Craven Motor Co.	High Street
South Elmsall	C. Wallis	4 Doncaster Road
Wakefield	T. F. Manby	258–262 Kirkgate

THE RALEIGH HANDBOOK

ISLANDS

Guernsey	W. J. Gray	38 and 40 Pollet Street, St. Peter Port
Isle of Man	A. F. Lawton	6 Arbory Street, Castletown
,,	Onchan Motors, Ltd.	Derby Square, Douglas
Isle of Wight	O. V. Mainstone	9 Union Street, Ryde
Jersey	Bissons	59 Halkett Place, St. Heliers

WALES

ANGLESEY—

Holyhead	M. Evans & Sons	Market Street
Llanfair P.G.	Wm. Jones	

BRECKNOCKSHIRE—

Brecon	Fryer Bros. & Co.
Talgarth	Fred T. Morgan

CARMARTHENSHIRE—

Carmarthen	W. Edwards & Son	Towy Garage

CARNARVONSHIRE—

Bangor	R. E. Grice	305 High Street
Chwilog	O. H. Griffith	Four Crosses
Llandudno	H. G. Nelson	Gloddaeth Avenue
Portmadoc	L. H. Thomas & Co.	
Pwllheli	R. J. Jones	Efailnewydd

DENBIGHSHIRE—

Denbigh	W. Edwards	The Garage
Ruthin	R. Beech & Sons	

FLINTSHIRE—

Rhyl	H. G. Nelson	The Garage

GLAMORGAN—

Bridgend	J. Lewis	Caroline Street
Cardiff	The Kennard Cycle Co.	20 City Road
Cowbridge	W. E. Jones	West End Garage, High Street
Pontardulais	Ben Morgan	
Pyle	R. T. Clarke	Central Garage
Swansea	Dan Morgan	218 Oxford Street

MERIONETHSHIRE—

Bala	E. Williams & Sons	

MONMOUTHSHIRE—

Blackwood	A. Chaston	Pentwyn Road
Newport	F. Turner	18 Clarence Place
Pontypool	A. Jelly	Osborne Road
Pontywain	T. Hayes	Midland Railway

PEMBROKESHIRE—

Pembroke	E. Davies	St. Michael's Square

SCOTLAND

ABERDEENSHIRE—

Aberdeen	D. C. Cruikshank	156 Union Street

SPARE PARTS STOCKISTS

AYRSHIRE—
Ayr	J. B. Neil	22 New Road
Maybole	R. Burns	70 High Street
Prestwick	W. N. Allan & Sons	St. Cuthbert's Garage, Main Street

BERWICKSHIRE—
Ayton	Hall's Garage, Ltd.	High Street
Berwick	Lion Garages, Ltd.	

DUMFRIESSHIRE—
Dumfries	Kirkpatrick Bros.	17 Waterloo Place
Eastriggs	W. J. Grieve	

DUMBARTONSHIRE—
Kirkintilloch	John McLay	43 High Street

ELGINSHIRE—
Elgin	G. Muir & Co	31 High Street

FIFESHIRE—
St. Andrews	Christie Bros.	Bridge Street

FORFARSHIRE—
Dundee	P. T. Jackson	31–35 Victoria Road
Montrose	Duthie & Son	52 High Street

INVERNESS-SHIRE—
Inverness	Alex. Munro	14–16 Falcon Square

KINCARDINESHIRE—
Laurencekirk	Tavendale & Son	High Street

KIRKCUDBRIGHTSHIRE—
Castle Douglas	W. Hamilton & Son	106 Cotton Street

LANARKSHIRE—
Glasgow	Alexander & Co.	272 Great Western Road
,,	Douglas Deans, Ltd	74 Great Western Road

MIDLOTHIAN—
Edinburgh	Alexander & Co.	115 Lothian Road

NAIRNSHIRE—
Nairn	Knowles & Cumming	9 Bridge Street

PERTHSHIRE—
Perth	D. Burns	64 George Street

ROSS AND CROMARTY—
Evanton	Kenneth MacKenzie	

ROXBURGHSHIRE—
Hawick	Milligan & Bell	7 Bridge Street
Jedburgh	R. Oliver	35 High Street

STIRLINGSHIRE—
Falkirk	C. J. Malley	61 Graham's Road

NORTHERN IRELAND

ANTRIM—
Belfast   J. C. Lamb   21 Church Street

DOWN—
Newtownards   R. A. M. Carse

FERMANAGH—
Enniskillen   John Jeffers   36 East Bridge Street

LONDONDERRY—
Londonderry   Patterson Bros.   4–5 John Street

IRISH FREE STATE

CORK—
Bantry   Kennedy & Co.   Bantry Garage

DUBLIN—
Dublin   J. J. Keating   32 and 33 Lower Abbey Street

LONGFORD—
Longford   W. & C. Pearce   Main Street

LOUTH—
Drogheda   P. Murphy, Ltd.   West Street
Dundalk   Thos. Williamson

MONAGHAN—
Monaghan   A. & D. Murphy   Glasslough Street

MEATH—
Navan   Navan Engineering Works   Watergate St.
Trim   Frank Pratt

WATERFORD—
Cappoquin   J. O'Keefe & Co.   Cappoquin Garage
Waterford   T. J. Sheridan   The Quay

WEXFORD—
Gore   N. Cooke   The Arcade

MAIN RALEIGH DEPOTS

(Carrying Comprehensive Stocks of Spare Parts)

LONDON: 33 FARRINGDON ROAD, E.C.1.
Telegrams : " Mospare, London." *Telephone :* 5120 Holborn.
(Above are fully equipped for carrying out minor repairs or complete overhauls.)

ABERDEEN	345 UNION STREET	Central 1123
BELFAST	104 ANN STREET	93
BIRMINGHAM	PARADISE STREET	Midland 858
BRISTOL	44 QUEEN'S ROAD, CLIFTON	3395
CORK	44 MacCURTAIN STREET	1419
BRISTOL (Branch)	26 OLD MARKET STREET	5019
DERBY	ST. PETER'S STREET	792
DUBLIN	5 LEINSTER STREET	1984
EDINBURGH	75 SHANDWICK PLACE	4844
HANLEY	53 PICCADILLY	888
HUDDERSFIELD	6 TRINITY STREET	739
LEEDS	58 VICAR LANE	27755
LEICESTER	DE MONTFORT HOUSE, LONDON ROAD	Central 1296
LIVERPOOL	45–49 BERRY STREET	Royal 2444
MANCHESTER	178–180 DEANSGATE	
NEWCASTLE-ON-TYNE	38 ST. MARY'S PLACE	Central 4489
NORWICH	22 PRINCE OF WALES ROAD	494
NOTTINGHAM	KING STREET	1576
OXFORD	106 ST. ALDATES	657
PLYMOUTH	171 UNION STREET	1602
SHEFFIELD	21 THE MOOR	Central 3862
SOUTHSEA	62 OSBORNE ROAD	Portsmouth 4662
SWINDON	THE SPOT, 60 REGENT STREET	119

GLOSSARY OF MOTOR-CYCLING TERMS

(*Numbers in brackets refer to pages in text*)

A.A. The Automobile Association, Fanum House, Whitcomb Street, W.C.2, a road organization offering many benefits to motor-cyclists who are members.

Accelerate. To quicken the speed of the machine by opening the throttle.

Accessory. Any part of the equipment of the machine not essential to its running.

Accumulator. Cells for storing electricity. Each cell consists of a set of lead plates and a set of peroxide plates, immersed in diluted sulphuric acid and contained in a celluloid case, fitted with terminals.

Acetylene. A gas (C_2H_2) used for lighting acetylene lamps, generated by allowing water to drip on to calcium carbide.

Acid. Familiar term used for the diluted sulphuric acid used in an accumulator. The correct proportions are one part of sulphuric acid to five parts of distilled water.

A.C.U. The Auto-Cycle Union, 83 Pall Mall, S.W.1, which is the governing body of the sporting side of motor-cycling, such as speed and reliability trials.

Adaptor. A fitting enabling a tyre pump of given size to fit any size valve.

Addendum. The height of a gear tooth above the pitch line.

Advance. Term used in relation to the timing of the spark. It is the distance at which spark occurs before piston reaches the top of its stroke or the number of degrees before the crankshaft reaches its highest position.

Air Leak. The connection from the carburettor to the inlet port may be loose, causing an air leak.

Air Lock. Air may find its way into the petrol pipe, its pressure preventing petrol from finding its way into the float chamber of the carburettor.

Air Slide. The sliding valve in the carburettor which controls the supply of air to the engine.

Alcohol. An organic hydro-carbon compound (C_2H_6O); in liquid form it is capable of being used to operate the engine in place of petrol, but owing to the high tax on it it is not generally used.

Ammeter. An instrument which indicates the number of amps. in an electrical circuit.

Amp. Abbreviation for ampere, the unit of measurement of the amount of current in an electrical circuit. The current produced by one volt in a circuit having a resistance of one ohm is one ampere.

Annealing. Various metal parts of a motor-cycle are annealed; this is done by heating the part and allowing it to cool very slowly.

Apron. The waterproof cloth between the windscreen and the sidecar body.

Armature. The iron core of the magneto; it is wound with insulated fine wire and rotates between the poles of the magnet.

GLOSSARY

Auto-ignition. Particles of carbon on the inside of the combustion chamber may become red-hot, thereby igniting the gas before the spark occurs and causing auto-ignition.

Automatic Valve. An inlet valve which is opened by the suction exerted by the descending piston, a light spring being fitted to close it again when the suction ceases. This type of valve is not used on the Raleigh motor-cycle, both the valves being mechanically operated.

Backfire. When starting the engine the momentum of the flywheel may be insufficient to overcome the increase in compression ratio caused by an early spark setting. The piston will be forced in the opposite direction and the rotation violently reversed.

Back Pressure. A choked silencer, or exhaust pipe of too small a diameter, hinders the burnt gases in their efforts to escape, causing back-pressure and overheating.

Baffle Plates. In some forms of silencer, plates with perforations are placed. These baffle plates cause the gases to make less noise when leaving the silencer.

Balance Weights. Weights formed of metal and attached to the crankshaft, to counterbalance the weight of the connecting rod and piston.

Ball Bearing. A bearing in which balls are inserted to allow the two surfaces to roll on the balls instead of sliding on each other. This decreases friction and heat, and increases life of bearing.

Ball Race. The grooved part of a ball bearing where the balls track.

Bearing. Where one piece of metal has to revolve inside or outside another, such as a wheel on its axle, the parts of the two metals which touch are termed a bearing. This may be a plain, ball, or roller bearing.

Bell Crank Lever. A right-angled piece of metal, used for transmitting push or pull at right-angles to the original line.

Belt. The driving belt between the gear-box pulley and rear wheel, composed of rubber and canvas, or occasionally leather.

Benzole. A by-product of coal gas, benzole (C_6H_6) may be used as a substitute for petrol.

Big End. The bearing at the lower end of the connecting rod.

Bore. The internal diameter of the cylinder, usually measured in millimetres. The bore forms the basis of the R.A.C. horse-power rating formula.

Bowden Wire. Wire composed of several strands and possessing greater flexibility and strength than a single wire of the same diameter.

Brake Drum. The drum attached to the rear wheel on which the brake operates.

Brake Horse-Power. The actual power developed at the pulley of the engine, found by applying a brake to the pulley. It may be calculated by the various formulae given in Chapter XII.

Brush. Usually refers to the piece of carbon held lightly by a spring to part of the rotating armature in the magneto, to collect the current.

Bush. The lining of a bearing, usually made of phosphor-bronze or white metal. When excessive wear has taken place it may be renewed.

Butt-end Tube. To replace an endless tube in a tyre it is necessary to remove the wheel. To save time and trouble, butt-end tubes are made, so that they may be inserted without removing the wheel.

Butterfly Nut. (*See* Wing Nut.)

Calcium Carbide. (CaC_2), when water is allowed to drip on to it, gives off acetylene gas.

Cam. A pear-shaped piece of metal rotating on a shaft, so that the projection will raise the valve at the correct moment.

Camber. The amount of vertical curve, or "hump," in the road.

Camshaft. The shaft to which the cam is secured.

Capacity. The capacity of an engine is usually reckoned in cubic centimetres and may be ascertained by the following formula—

$$c.c. = D^2 \times .7854 \times S \times N$$

(D = diameter of cylinder in centimetres; S = stroke in centimetres; N = number of cylinders).

Carbide. Familiar term for calcium carbide.

Carbon. The deposit formed inside the cylinder, caused by burnt particles of dust and oil. Another form of carbon is the material of which the carbon brush of the magneto is made.

Carburation. The work of transforming liquid petrol into a gas, performed by the carburettor.

Carburettor. The device which transforms liquid petrol into a gas and mixes a suitable proportion of air with the gas before it is admitted to the cylinder.

Case-Hardening. Valves, bearing surfaces, cones, and other parts of a motor-cycle which have to be extremely hard are case-hardened by their being heated for a considerable time, up to six hours, according to the use to which they are to be put. They are then allowed to cool, reheated to a dull red heat, and plunged into oil or cold water, with the result that the surface is hardened more than the interior.

Castellated Shaft. A shaft with longitudinal grooves, such as the shaft to which the gear-box pulley is attached and the shafts in the gear-box on which the gear-wheels slide.

Castings. Cylinders, etc., are first made by molten metal being run into suitable moulds. This gives them their rough shape and they are afterwards machined with great accuracy to their correct dimensions.

Cast Iron. Iron which is used for casting, such as in the manufacture of cylinders. It is so called because it is run into casts or moulds.

C.C. Abbreviation for cubic capacity.

Change Lever. The lever by which the gears are changed from one speed to another.

Chassis. The metal framework from which the sidecar is suspended.

Choke Tube. A smaller tube placed inside the tube from the carburettor in which the air and gas are mixed in order to increase the air velocity past the jet.

Clutch. The device by which the power from the front chain is transmitted to the gear-box. It consists of sets of plates, alternately connected to gear-box sprocket and front chain sprocket, and held together by springs. The springs can be released so that the plates do not grip each other, thereby allowing the engine to run "free."

Clutch Lever. The lever by which the clutch springs are released, so that the clutch may be engaged or disengaged at will.

Clutch Sprocket. The gear-wheel on which the chain from engine to gear-box runs, at the gear-box.

Coasting. When running downhill the machine may be put in neutral gear, thus "coasting" down the hill without engine power.

Combination. Term for motor-cycle with sidecar attached.

Combustion Chamber. The space inside the cylinder above the top of the piston where the explosion takes place.

GLOSSARY

Compensator. Dog clutches can engage only when their teeth are in the correct positions to engage with each other, so that, in a gear-box, a "compensator" is placed, consisting of a spring which will engage them when they are ready. Its purpose is to prevent damage by rough handling.

Compression. The downward stroke of the piston draws a charge of gas into the cylinder; the next stroke upwards then compresses it, in order to mix it more completely and to effect a more forcible explosion. Although a considerable amount of energy is used up in this compression stroke, it is more than compensated by the extra power gained.

Compression Ratio. Refers to the proportion of space filled by compressed mixture compared with the space it fills before the compression stroke takes place.

Compression Tap. The tap on the top of the cylinder head, which may be opened to inject petrol from the priming tap.

Condenser. As its name implies, the contact breaker breaks the current in the primary coil of the magneto, thereby causing a current in the secondary coil and a spark at the sparking plug. This sudden breaking of current would tend to cause a spark to jump across the points of the contact breaker and to prevent this a condenser is fitted across the contact breaker. When the primary circuit is broken charges of current pile up on the platinum points of the contact breaker, and to prevent the current jumping the gap it passes into the condenser, a device capable of holding a small charge of current for a short time.

Cone. The term applied to the ball races in the wheel bearings. They are cone-shaped, circular pieces of case-hardened metal holding the balls in place, and may be adjusted to the correct tightness as required.

Conk Out. Familiar term meaning to breakdown.

Connecting Rod. The part of the engine joining the piston to the crankshaft, thereby transforming the up and down motion of the piston into the circular motion of the flywheel.

Conrod. Familiar term for connecting rod.

Contact Breaker. In a magneto the current is generated, as shown under "Magneto," in the primary circuit and has to be broken to obtain a spark at the sparking plug. The contact breaker revolves, and at a certain point a depression in its casing allows a spring to separate the points, thus breaking the circuit.

Control Lever. Term applied to each of the various levers on the machine used for regulating it.

Convertible Combination. The sidecar with an additional folding seat at the rear of the permanent seat, so that it may accommodate two passengers instead of one if required.

Copper Asbestos Washer. Copper and asbestos both being capable of withstanding a great amount of heat, washers are made with a lining of copper and inside of asbestos, and used for parts of the engine which have to withstand great heat, such as packing between the cylinder and cylinder head.

Cork Inserts. To enable the clutch plates to grip each other more readily, circular pieces of cork are inserted in alternate plates. Occasionally Ferodo inserts are used in place.

Coslettizing. In order to render the frame and enamelled parts of a motorcycle rustproof, the metal is subjected to a treatment known as coslettizing, which renders it rustproof. Several coats of paint and enamel are then applied.

Cotter. The flat pin which goes through the base of the valve-stem to keep the valve spring in position.

Countershaft Gear. A gear, such as the Sturmey-Archer on the Raleigh,

THE RALEIGH HANDBOOK

where the gear-wheels are placed on more than one shaft, as opposed to the hub or epicyclic gear, which all work on a common shaft.

Cover. The outside part of the tyre, often needlessly named the "outer" cover.

Crank. The shaft to which the lower end of the connecting rod is connected. Any shaft which has an arm formed of two right-angles on it is termed a crank.

Crankcase. The aluminium case in which the crankshaft revolves.

Crankshaft. The shaft on which the flywheel is fitted and which transmits the power from the connecting rod to the flywheel.

Crash. Familiar term for an accident.

Crash-helmet. Special helmet of leather with hard dome, to prevent injury to head in case of accident.

Cubic Capacity. (*See* Capacity.)

Cush Drive. Familiar term for the work performed by the shock absorber, which smooths the jerkiness of the drive.

Cut-out. A cut-out is means whereby the exhaust gases are allowed to escape into the open air instead of passing through the exhaust pipe and silencer. It is illegal to use one in this country.

Cylinder. The tubular part of the engine in which the piston moves up and down.

Cylinder Head. In the case of an overhead valve engine, the top portion of the cylinder is removable and is termed the cylinder head.

Dead Centre. When the piston is exactly at the top or bottom of its stroke it is said to be at dead centre.

Decarbonize. To decarbonize an engine is to remove the carbon which collects on the inside of the cylinder walls and top of the piston.

De-coke. Familiar term for decarbonize.

Distilled Water. The water which should be used for filling an accumulator, as it contains less impurities than common water. It is made by turning water into steam, which is then condensed, i.e. turned into water again, leaving its impurities behind.

Distributor. A piece of apparatus whereby one magneto may supply sparks to more than one sparking plug on a multi-cylinder engine. A revolving part makes contact at the correct moment with a terminal leading to the particular sparking plug which needs a spark. Different terminals lead to different plugs, so that each may be supplied in turn.

Dog Clutch. A form of positive drive whereby two members, each having jaws, slide together and are interlocked.

Double Clutching. When changing from a high gear to a lower one, the gear is put in neutral and the clutch let in, thus speeding up the layshaft and ensuring a gear-change which is more silent and involves less wear on the gear-box. This is hardly necessary on a motor-cycle and refers more to car practice.

Down Tube. The tube of the frame leading from beneath the head lug to the crankcase.

Drain Plug. The plug at the bottom of the crankcase which may be removed to drain off oil.

Drip Feed. An arrangement whereby the oil is fed to the engine drip by drip, thus ensuring a more even supply than when a charge is injected by a pump at intervals.

Dynamo. A machine for generating electricity. The working is similar

GLOSSARY

that of a magneto (q.v.) except that a continuous charge of current is given and the primary circuit is not broken for the purpose of procuring a spark.

Dynamometer. An instrument used for measuring power, used to test the power given out by engines before they are assembled in the frames.

Earth. In many electrical and telegraph systems the earth is used as a return path for the current, for the sake of economy and simplicity. In the case of a motor-cycle the frame is used as a return path for the current from the sparking plug back to the magneto, and is termed an "earth."

Electrolyte. The mixture of sulphuric acid and distilled water contained within the cells of an accumulator.

Endorsements. The record of convictions entered on the back of a driving licence.

Exhaust. The burnt gases which are expelled from the engine.

Exhaust Lifter. A lever which lifts the exhaust valve and keeps it raised, with the result that the gas escapes from the cylinder through the exhaust valve port before it is exploded.

Exhaust Pipe. The pipe connecting the exhaust port to the silencer.

Exhaust Port. The passage round the exhaust valve through which the burnt gases escape from the cylinder.

Exhaust Stroke. The stroke during which the piston is travelling upwards in the cylinder while the exhaust valve is open to expel the burnt gases.

Exhaust Valve. The valve which is mechanically operated to open and liberate the burnt gases after they have been exploded in the cylinder.

Explosion Stroke. The stroke during which the piston is forced downwards in the cylinder by the power of the explosion of gas.

Feeler Gauge. On the side of the magneto spanner is a thin strip of steel termed the feeler gauge, and used for gauging the distance between the platinum points of the contact breaker.

Ferodo Inserts. To enable the plates of a clutch to grip each other more securely, inserts of Ferodo are placed in the alternate plates. Cork is sometimes used for this purpose.

Filament. The wire, usually of platinum or tungsten, inside the electric bulb of the lamp which glows white-hot when an electric current is passed along it.

Filler Cap. The caps screwed on the petrol and oil tanks.

Filters. The fine gauze meshes placed to catch dirt in the petrol on its way from petrol tank to carburettor.

Fins. To assist cooling, the cylinder is cast with fins on it, to increase the area of its surface and thus assist radiation of heat.

Fishtail. The attachment to the extreme end of the exhaust pipe, so that the gases escape through a narrow slot instead of from the circular pipe.

Flapper-bracket. Familiar term for the carrier.

Flashpoint. The degree of heat at which oil burns. A good oil possesses a higher flashpoint than one of low grade.

Flexible Shaft. Usually refers to the flexible cable which forms the drive for the speedometer.

Float. The hollow and air-tight piece of metal inside the float chamber of the carburettor. It floats on the petrol, and when sufficient petrol is admitted to the chamber raises the needle and cuts off further supply, preventing flooding.

Float Chamber. The part of the carburettor containing the float.

Flooding. If the needle in the carburettor does not effectively control the supply of petrol, flooding will take place. In starting the engine, the carburettor may be purposely flooded to ensure a full supply of petrol to the engine.

Flywheel. The heavy wheel secured to the crankshaft. Its momentum carries the engine over the three strokes on which no power is transmitted.

Footboards. The boards on which the rider rests his feet.

Footrests. Supplied for the same purpose as footboards, but preferred by most riders as footrests give a more positive grip of the machine.

Forced Circulation. The action of a piece of apparatus such as an oil-pump, forcing the oil through engine, as opposed to oiling which depends on gravity.

Four-stroke Engine. The type of engine which has one power stroke in every four strokes of the piston. The strokes are named in order—inlet stroke, compression stroke, power stroke, and exhaust stroke (q.v.).

Frame. The tubular part of the motor-cycle carrying the engine, petrol tank, gear-box, etc.

French Chalk. White chalk used for preventing the tube sticking to the cover after a patch has been stuck on the tube and it has been replaced in the cover. It is also generally used inside the cover to prevent friction and wear on the tube.

Fulcrum. A pivot on which a lever works, such as the gear-change lever.

Fuse. A piece of fine wire included in an electrical circuit, so that in the event of a short-circuit or too much current being put through the circuit the fuse will break down and thus save lamps, etc., from damage.

Gadget. Familiar term applied to anything.

Gas. Term used for the explosive mixture used in the engine.

Gate Change. A gear-change lever which has positive stops in each position.

Gear-box. The mechanism for increasing or decreasing the proportion of the engine speed in relation to wheel speed. On a low gear the engine speed is greater in proportion than on a high gear at the same wheel speed.

Gear Ratio. The proportion of engine revolutions to wheel revolutions. Thus, if the wheel performs 500 revolutions per minute and the engine 2,500, the gear ratio is said to be 5 to 1.

Generator. The vessel used to mix water with calcium carbide, forming acetylene gas for lighting purposes.

Gradient. Term used in describing the slope of a hill. A hill which rises 1 ft. in 5 ft. of travel is said to have a gradient of 1 in 5.

Gravity Feed. A supply of petrol to the carburettor is ensured by placing the petrol tank above the carburettor, thus depending on the action of gravity.

Grinding In. After much use valves become worn and do not fit their seatings so well as formerly. They have then to be " ground in," to restore their non-leaking properties.

Ground Clearance. The distance from the lowest point of the machine (except the wheels) to the ground.

Grub Screw. A small screw without any head, but merely a slot cut in it.

Gudgeon Pin. The pin in the piston to which the little end of the connecting rod is attached. Usually it is free to rotate both in the piston and the little end.

Guides. The tubes in which the valves and tappets slide up and down.

Gusset Plate. A flat metal plate placed at junctions of the frame and crankcase to strengthen the frame and prevent side-to-side play.

Hairpin. Familiar term for a sharp corner shaped like a hairpin.

GLOSSARY

Half-time Shaft. Term used for the cam shaft, which rotates at half engine speed.

Head. The part of the frame where the steering column is housed.

High Gear. The gear on which the number of wheel revolutions compared with engine revolutions is higher than when it is on other gears.

Horse-power. Strictly speaking, 1 horse-power is the energy required to raise 33,000 lb. 1 ft. high in 1 min. For calculating motor-cycle engine horse-power, a unit of power is used, termed "brake horse-power" (q.v.).

H.T. Wire. The wire which conveys the electric current from the magneto to the sparking plug.

Hub Gear. A type of gear, now obsolete, working on the epicyclic principle, and contained in the hub of the rear wheel.

Ignition. Term used to describe the act of exploding the charge of gas in the cylinder.

Inlet Pipe. The pipe through which gas passes on its way from the carburettor to the inlet port.

Inlet Port. The passage round the inlet valve through which the gas passes into the cylinder.

Inlet Stroke. The stroke during which the downward movement of piston exerts suction which draws in a fresh charge of gas through the inlet valve and port.

Inlet Valve. The valve which is mechanically operated at the correct moment to allow gas to pass into the cylinder.

Inner Tube. Term applied to the tube of a tyre.

Insulation. To prevent electric current from escaping from a wire, the latter is wrapped round with insulating tape or some non-conducting material such as rubber.

Internal Combustion Engine. Term used to describe the motor-cycle engine, so called because heat is applied inside the cylinder, as opposed to an external combustion engine, such as the steam engine, where the heat is applied outside the cylinder.

Internal Expanding Brake. A brake which works by means of pressure being applied to the inner circumference of a drum, as opposed to an external contracting brake, which works on the outside circumference of the drum.

Jack. An implement for lifting heavy weights, used for cars and usually unnecessary for motor-cycles, although useful when repairing a sidecar wheel puncture.

Jet. The finely-bored tube through which petrol passes in the carburettor. Its object is to pass the petrol in a fine stream, thereby assisting vaporization.

Journal. The surface of the inner member of a bearing, or, more strictly, the entire inner member.

Juice. Familiar term for petrol, or, electrically speaking, for electricity.

Key. A tapered piece of metal which secures a flywheel, for instance, on its shaft.

Key-way. The groove in which a key fits.

Kick-starter. The arm attached to the gear-box for the purpose of rotating the engine.

Knee-grips. Rubber pads attached to the sides of the petrol tank to assist the rider in controlling and gripping the machine.

Knocking. The metallic noise heard when an engine is running slowly and is overloaded.

Lap. One circuit of a race-track is termed a lap.

Lateral Thrust. Pressure applied at the side, such as the pressure a cam would apply to a valve were no rocker-arm interposed.

Lay-shaft. The shaft of the gear-box to which the two sprockets are not connected ; the shaft which runs idly when the machine is in neutral gear.

Leg-shields. Shields of pressed metal attached to the frame to keep the elements, road-dust, etc., from the rider's legs.

Liquid Brazing. To ensure perfect junction at the angles of the frame they are immersed in a bath of molten brass, which forms a more perfect joint than with ordinary brazing.

Little End. The end of the connecting rod which is attached, by means of the gudgeon pin, to the piston.

Lock Nut. A nut placed over another on the same thread to prevent the original nut working loose.

Low Gear. The gear in which wheel revolutions in proportion to engine revolutions are at their lowest.

Machining. After various parts of a motor-cycle have been cast, they are carefully machined down to their correct size and weight. The cylinder of a Raleigh, for instance, when cast weighs 17 lb. and after machining 13 lb.

Magdyno. A special form of dynamo which generates current for the electric lighting system as well as for the ignition system.

Magnet. A horse-shoe shaped piece of metal in the magneto which exerts a magnetic influence.

Magnetic Field. The space over which the magnetic influence of the magnet is exerted.

Magneto. A form of dynamo which supplies electricity for the magneto. The armature revolves within the magnetic field, causing a current of electricity to flow in its primary winding. This is broken by the contact breaker, and by induction this causes a current to flow in the secondary circuit, which passes on to the sparking plug, causing a spark which ignites the gas.

Make-and-break. Another term for the contact breaker.

Misfire. Term used when the gas is not exploded for some reason. It enters and leaves the cylinder without being exploded.

Mixture. Term used to denote the gas formed from petrol and vapour and air being mixed.

M.M. Abbreviation for millimetre.

M.P.G. Miles per gallon.

M.P.H. Miles per hour.

Muffler. Term for silencer.

Multiple Disc Clutch. A clutch, such as that in the Sturmey-Archer gear, which consists of a number of plates.

Naphtha. A volatile bituminous liquid, a by-product of coal gas, which can be used instead of petrol.

Needle. The part in the carburettor float chamber which shuts off the supply of petrol when the float chamber is full.

Negative Pole. The lead plates of the accumulator form the negative side, and is the side to which the current returns after passing through lamps.

Nickel Steel. An alloy of nickel and steel, usually about 4 per cent of nickel to 96 per cent of steel, used for valve manufacturing purposes owing to its hardness and capabilities for withstanding metallic "fatigue."

Nipple. Special attachments to the forks, etc., to which the grease gun is affixed for lubrication purposes.

GLOSSARY

O.H.V. Term for overhead valve.

Oil Ducts. Grooves cut in bearings to assist lubrication.

Otto Cycle. Term for the four-stroke engine (q.v.).

Outer Cover. Term used to denote the cover of a tyre.

Outfit. Term applied to a combination.

Overhead Valve. A valve which is placed above the cylinder, opposed to side-by-side valves at the side of the cylinder.

Overheating. Term used when the engine has become too hot, due to lack of lubrication, overload, or other causes.

Oxygen Process. The process of decarbonization whereby the carbon is removed by an oxygen flame being directed on it. The oxygen consumes the carbon, thus making decarbonization easier than by the older method of removing the cylinder and scraping.

Packing. Material placed between the two surfaces of a joint, such as the copper asbestos washer placed between a cylinder and cylinder head.

Parallel Wiring. Term used when the lamps are taken from a battery in parallel, i.e. each lamp is on a separate circuit, as opposed to series winding, when the circuit goes from one lamp to the next. The advantage is that if one lamp fails, with parallel wiring, the others keep working.

Parking Place. A special stand in a crowded area where a motor-cycle may be left.

Pawl. A catch, held by a spring, which allows a ratchet to rotate in one direction only, used on a motor-cycle in conjunction with the kick-starter.

Petrol. A liquid distilled from mineral oil, used generally for motor-cycles. It has a specific gravity of about ·7 ; 1 gall. of petrol weighs about $7\frac{1}{2}$ lb. and 1 cu. in. of petrol yields about 275 cu. in. of petrol gas. Its freezing point is − 180° Fahrenheit, and when exploded in the cylinder reaches a temperature often over 1,000° Centigrade.

Phospher Bronze. An alloy of bronze used in bearings.

Pillion Rider. Term used for a passenger riding on the carrier.

Pin. Term referring to gudgeon pin, crank-pin, taper-pin, or split pin, all of which are used in various parts of a motor-cycle.

Pinion. When two gear wheels are in mesh the smaller is termed the pinion. Also used with reference to any small gear-wheel.

Pinking. Familiar term for knocking.

Piston. The medium through which the expansion of the gas is conveyed to the connecting rod and thence converted to a rotary motion. It is usually of cup-shaped formation, lightly constructed of cast-iron or aluminium alloy.

Piston Ring. A cast-iron ring fitting in grooves round the piston, to ensure a tight fit in the cylinder walls and to prevent gas blowing downwards past the piston.

Piston Speed. May be calculated by multiplying the number of engine revolutions per minute by two and then by the length of the stroke. This gives the speed per minute. The Raleigh engine has a stroke of 88 mm. ; this is approximately $3\frac{1}{2}$ in., so that if the engine is running at 5,000 revolutions per minute, the number of inches travelled in 1 min. will be 35,000—nearly 34 miles per hour. This is, of course, the total distance travelled by the piston—not the uniform speed, as it has to " stop and turn " twice in each revolution.

Pitch. The pitch of a chain is the distance from the centre of one link to the centre of the next ; on a gear-wheel the distance from a point on one tooth to a corresponding point on the next.

Pitting. The holes which appear on the surface of valves are termed pitting.

Plain Bearing. One where the two surfaces slide over each other, as opposed to a ball or roller bearing.

Plate Clutch. A clutch, such as the Sturmey-Archer, which consists of plates running concentrically.

Platinum Points. As platinum is able to withstand great heat and is a good conductor of electricity, it is used for the points of the contact breaker.

Plug. Familiar term for sparking plug.

Plug Points. Term for the points of the sparking plug where the spark occurs.

Poles. The term applied to the ends of a horse-shoe magnet ; also to the terminals of a battery.

Poppet Valve. Another term for mushroom valve, the type used in the Raleigh engine.

Popping. Term used when the gas explodes or pops back into the carburettor.

Ports. The passages where the inlet and exhaust valves of the engine are housed.

Positive Pole. The lead peroxide plates of the accumulator form the positive side, from which the current flows to the lamps.

Pot-holes. Familiar term applied to large holes made in the road surface by heavy traffic.

Power Stroke. The stroke during which the exploding gas sends the piston forcibly to the bottom of its stroke.

Pre-ignition. Carbon deposits on the piston and cylinder heads become red-hot and ignite the gas before the spark occurs. May also be caused by unsuitable plug, the points of which become incandescent.

Premium. The amount paid to the insurance company to secure a policy.

Primary Battery. A battery capable of generating electricity by chemical action, as opposed to a secondary battery, such as an accumulator, which can merely store electricity.

Primary Circuit. The circuit of the magneto in which the current is first induced.

Primary Drive. Term applied to the drive from engine to gear-box.

Priming. Term applied to injection of petrol through the compression tap into the cylinder to effect easy starting.

Pulley. The belt-pulley of V-section, on which the belt runs, at the gear-box.

Push Rod. The rod which operates an overhead valve, situated between the tappet and the valve rocker.

R.A.C. The Royal Automobile Club, Pall Mall, S.W.1, which offers many advantages to motor-cyclists who are members.

Race. Term used to denote running an engine at excessive speeds when not under load. It is harmful to the engine, as undue vibration is caused.

Ratchet. A toothed wheel cut so that a pawl can be used in conjunction with it, to permit its revolving in one direction only.

Re-faced Valves. After valves have been worn through their case-hardened surface, it is advisable to send them back to the works to be " re-faced."

Registration. The act of giving the authorities the necessary particulars regarding a motor-cycle, for the purpose of issuing a licence and number, etc.

Registration Book. The book in which these particulars are entered. One book is issued for each motor-cycle.

GLOSSARY

Retard. When the spark is timed to occur behind its normal time it is said to be retarded.

Revving. Familiar term for an engine running at great speed.

Rocker. The arm, pivoted in the centre, which transmits the power from the push rod to the stem of the valve. This is used in conjunction with overhead valves only. Also the lever between the cam and the base of the valve stem, interposed to prevent excessive wear and side-thrust.

Roller Bearing. Similar to a ball bearing, but one in which rollers are used in place of balls.

Roller Chain. A motor-cycle driving chain consists of links and rollers which turn when in contact with the sprocket teeth, thus eliminating friction.

R.P.M. Revolutions per minute.

Run-in. An engine is said to be " run-in " after it has run about 500 miles ; by this time the bearings have acquired a glass-hard surface.

Scoring. The cylinder walls may be " scored," if a piston or piston-ring breaks, by the sharp edges scraping grooves in the walls.

Seating. The base on which the valve face rests.

Seat-pillar. The tube supporting the saddle which enters the frame of the motor-cycle.

Secondary Battery. A battery, such as an accumulator, which is not capable of generating electricity, but only of storing it, as opposed to a primary battery, which is capable of generating electricity.

Secondary Circuit. The circuit of the magneto into which the current is induced when the primary circuit is broken by the contact breaker. The secondary circuit supplies the current directly to the sparking plug.

Security Bolts. Bolts, usually two in number, placed through the rim of the wheel for the purpose of holding the cover more securely on the rim.

Seizing. When a piston or bearing becomes overheated from lack of lubrication or other cause it binds and is said to have seized.

Selector Rod. The rod inside the gear-box which changes the positions of the gear-wheels to engage different gears.

Semi-sports Model. A machine designed for use as a sporting mount as well as a touring mount. Usually considered faster than a touring machine, but not claiming to be equal to a sports model.

Series Wiring. The system when the electric current runs from the accumulator to each lamp in turn and then back to the accumulator, as opposed to parallel wiring, when it runs to each lamp separately.

Shock Absorber. A device which takes up any jerkiness in the drive, usually consisting of rubber buffers incorporated in the clutch sprocket, or rear wheel.

Short-circuit. A current short-circuits when it is able to return to its source without passing along its proper path, as when the insulation of a wire is rubbed through and it touches the frame or another wire.

Shunt Wiring. Another term for parallel wiring.

Side-by-side Valves. Valves which are placed at the side of the cylinder are said to be side-by-side valves, as opposed to overhead valves, which are over the cylinder.

Sight Feed. An oil feed which allows the rate of flow to be visible, usually through a cylinder of glass.

Silencer. A pressed steel or aluminium box through which the exhaust gases pass, to lessen the noise of their explosion.

Skirt. The lower cylindrical wall of a piston is termed the skirt.

Slides. The valves in the carburettor which control the amount of air and petrol gas admitted to the cylinder.

Small End. The end of the connecting rod connected to the piston by means of the gudgeon pin.

Solder. An alloy of two parts of lead to one of tin, used for joining various metals where great strength is not needed.

Solo. A motor-cycle without a sidecar attached.

Sooting-up. Term used to denote an engine in which excessive carbon accumulation is forming.

Sparking Plug. The device by which a spark is made to occur inside the cylinder. It consists of a metal centre-piece surrounded by insulation, usually porcelain or mica, which is also surrounded by another metal core. Points from the outside core nearly touch the central electrode, leaving a small gap across which the spark jumps.

Speedometer. An instrument for measuring the distance travelled by a motor-cycle and the number of miles per hour at which it travels.

Spigot. The lower end of the cylinder which fits inside the crankcase.

Splash Lubrication. The system whereby lubrication is effected by oil being splashed on to the moving parts. In the case of the motor-cycle engine, the big end bearing dips into oil which is forced into the crankcase by the mechanical oil pump and splashes it on to the cylinder walls and piston.

Sports Model. A motor-cycle designed essentially for speed.

Sprayer. The circular piece of metal inside the carburettor which further breaks up the petrol vapour and helps mixture.

Spring Washer. A washer, of spiral shape, which exerts pressure on the nut above it and so prevents the nut from working loose.

Sprocket. A toothed wheel designed for a chain-drive, as opposed to a gear-wheel, which is designed to engage with other gear-wheels.

Staggered Spokes. The motor-cycle wheel spokes are staggered, i.e. do not run directly from the centre of the axle, but run tangentially from the sides of the hub.

Stamping. A stamping is a small motor-cycle component part, such as the hub, which is stamped from a piece of sheet steel.

Stands. The tubular legs by which a motor-cycle wheel may be held off the ground.

Steering Column. The tubular column connecting the handlebar to the front fork, enabling the front wheel to be turned to the right or left.

Stoving. In order to harden enamel and to give it a fine polished appearance, enamel is " stoved " in ovens after being applied.

Stripping. A bolt is said to be stripped when its thread has been forcibly torn off it. A nut can also be stripped in the same manner.

Stroke. The length of travel of the piston.

Stunt. A feat involving skill, nerve and luck.

Sulphuric Acid. An acid which, when mixed with distilled water, forms the electrolyte of an accumulator.

Sump. A trough which holds oil, into which some moving part dips.

Tappet. A metal rod raised by a rotating cam, or rocker, conveying the latter's movement to the valve.

GLOSSARY

Tappet Guide. The bush or sleeve in which the tappet moves up and down (p. 53).

Tension. Is direct pulling stress, such as that applied to a motor-cycle belt or chain.

Throttle. The slide in the carburettor which controls the supply of petrol vapour to the engine.

Tickling. To assist easy starting the needle of the carburettor may be raised or depressed to cause the petrol to overflow the top of the jet. This operation is known as tickling, or flooding.

Timing Gear. Name given to the gear-wheels which operate the cams and magneto, causing the valves to open and close and the spark to occur at the correct moments.

Top Dead Centre. When the piston is exactly at the top of its stroke, it is said to be at top dead centre.

Top Gear. The same as high gear.

Top Tube. The tube of the frame above the tank.

Torque. The turning effect on a shaft.

Touring Model. A motor-cycle in which speed is not the only consideration, general efficiency, economy, and comfort being also catered for.

Transmission. Term applied to the parts of the machine embodying the drive from engine sprocket to gear-box and thence to the back wheel.

Tube. The inside part of a tyre, often needlessly named the " inner " tube.

Tuning. The art of obtaining maximum efficiency from an engine.

Twin. A motor-cycle engine with two cylinders.

Twistgrip. A form of control by means of which the throttle is operated and the ignition advanced and retarded by means of handlebar grips which can be twisted. A popular form of control in the Colonies and abroad.

Two-stroke Engine. An engine in which one power stroke is delivered every second stroke, as opposed to the four-stroke principle on which all Raleigh engines work.

Tyre Gauge. An instrument for measuring, in lbs., pressure to the square inch, the air pressure inside the tube.

Union. Usually applied to the joint of the carburettor and inlet port, but may refer to any joint.

Valances. The flaps on the sides of the mudguard to prevent mud from being splashed on to the rider.

Valves. Usually made of nickel steel and provided to permit the ingress and egress of the gases to and from the combustion chamber.

Valve Face. The surface of the valve which comes in contact with the seating.

Valve Grinding. After considerable use the valve face becomes pitted and needs to be " ground in," i.e. trued up exactly to fit its seating.

Valve Guide. The bushed part of the valve port in which the valve slides up and down.

Valve Lift. The distance a valve is raised from its seating.

Valve Port. The part of the cylinder containing the valve.

Valve Rocker. A piece of case-hardened metal, pivoted in its centre, which transmits the action of the push rod to the stem of the valve, in an overhead-valve engine.

Valve Seating. The surface of the valve port which comes in contact with the valve face.

Variable Jet. A jet capable of adjustment, so that it will pass a greater or lesser amount of petrol at the rider's will.

Volt. The unit of electrical pressure. One volt is needed to cause a current of one ampere in a circuit having a resistance of one ohm. One accumulator cell, when charged, should give at least 1·8 volts, and when it falls below this figure needs recharging.

Voltmeter. An instrument for measuring voltage.

V-rim. The rim on the front wheel in which the brake shoe operates. It also applies to the belt-pulley on the rear wheel.

Vulcanizing. A form of tyre repairing. Rubber and sulphur are mixed in correct proportions and applied to the tube to be repaired and subjected to heat and pressure.

Watt. Volts multiplied by amperes give watts. Thus a dynamo giving a current of 6 volts at 3 amps. causes a current of 18 watts; 760 watts equal 1 horse-power.

Welding. The process of heating metals to melting point, so that the two parts will unite.

Winding. The wire wound round the armature of a magneto is termed the primary winding. The other circuit in the magneto is termed the secondary winding.

Wing Nut. A nut having wings to enable it to be screwed with the fingers.

INDEX

ABROAD, touring 85
Absorber, shock, 20
Accident, what to do in case of, 91
Accumulator, care of, 70
Address, refusing, 92
Air leaks, 49
—— lock, 49
Aligning sidecar, 72
Aluminium piston, 75
Amal carburettor described, 17
Animals, unattended, on road, 42
Appeal, right of, 94
Approach, warning of, 93
Arrest, 93
Auto-Cycle Union, 31
Automobile Association, 31

BRAKE adjustments, 69
Brakes, 23
——, use of, 37
Brooks saddle, 24
Buying new machine 8
—— second-hand machine, 97

CABLE, high-tension, defective, 52
Cables, broken, 50
Carbon brush, defective, 52
——, removing from engine, 56
Carburettor, Amal, 17
——, " popping back " in, 55
——, principle of, 14
—— troubles, 49
Careful driving, 42
Chain, adjusting front, 68
——, magneto, adjusting, 69
——, rear, adjusting, 68
Chains, care of, 67, 76
Cleaning the machine, 73
Clothes for touring, 81, 86
Club, joining, 30
Clubs—
    Auto-Cycle Union, 31

Clubs (cont.)—
    Automobile Association, 31
    Raleigh Motor-Cycle Club, 31
    Royal Automobile Club, 31
Clutch, operating, 38
——, parts, 19
Combination outfit, driving, 38
——, making left-hand turn with, 39
Combinations, 7, 8, 9
Compensator, 19
Competition riding, 77
Confidence, 43
Connecting rod broken, 48
Contact breaker, trouble with, 51
Continental touring, 85
Controls, action of, 33
——, engine, 33
Corner, how to take, 39
——, sign, 39
Corners and cross roads, 39
Countershaft gear, 19
Crankcase, cleaning, 62
Connecting rod broken, 48
Cross roads and corners, 39
Cush drive, purpose of, 19

DANGEROUS corner sign, 95
Decarbonizing engine, 56
Detachable wheel, 45
Dismantling engine, 57
Dress, choice of, 81, 86
Drive, cush, 19
Driving hints, 36
——, furious, 93
—— in traffic, 41
—— licence, 28

ELECTRIC lamps, wiring, 71
Enamelling, 74
Engine controls, 33
——, cut-away view of, 15
——, decarbonizing, 56
——, elements of, 12
——, how it works, 12

INDEX

Engine, lubricating, 19, 38
——, overhead valve, 4, 6
——, procedure after starting, 35
——, re-assembling, 62
——, revolutions, 102
——, side valve described, 1
——, starting, 35
——, stops, 46
——, strokes of, 13
—— troubles, 46
——, types of, 12
Equivalent speeds, 101
Exhaust, colour of, 55
—— lifter, abuse of, 54
—— pipe, 24
—— valve lifter, 33

FAULTS, locating, 46
Flywheel, function of, 14
Forks, adjusting and lubricating, 67
Four-stroke engine, elements of, 12
—— ——, principle of, 12

GEAR-BOX, 18
Gear changing, 36
—— ratios for models, 5, 7
——, three-speed countershaft, 19
——, operating, 35
Glossary of motor-cycling terms, 115
Goggles, choice of, 81, 89
Gradients, table of, 101
Gudgeon pin, 61

HANDLEBAR controls, 34
Hand signalling, 39
Hats, 89
High-tension cable, defective, 52
Hill climbing, 37
Hire purchase, 26
Horns, law regarding, 28
Horse-power, calculating, 102
Horses, led, 41
Hotels, 83

IGNITION timing, 64
—— troubles, 50
Illumination, law regarding, 96
Inlet valve timing, 64
Insurance, 29

JET, choked, 49
Joints, making, 62
——, making washers for, 62

KICK-STARTER, using, 35
Knocking, 36

LADIES, motor-cycling for, 86
Lamps, 70
——, electric, wiring, 71
——, maintenance, 70
Leaks, plug and compression tap, 79
Left, turning to, 39
Legal hints, 91
Leg shields, 83
Licence, driving, 28
——, endorsement of, 92
Lighting-up time-table, 103
Lubricating the engine, 19, 38
Lubrication system, 19
—— details, 19
Luggage, 81

MAGNETO chain, adjusting, 68
—— contact breaker, trouble with, 51
——, how driven, 17
——, principle of, 17
——, rocker arm sticking, 51
—— timing, 64
Make-and-break, action of, 17
Maps, 85
Mechanical oil pump, 21
Motor-cycling for ladies, 86

NIGHT riding, 42
Number plate, rules regarding, 27
—— plates, 27

OIL supply, adjusting, 38
Overhauling, 56
——, general points, 64
Overhead valve engine, 5
—— —— model, 2¾ h.p., 5
Overheating, 52

PAPER washers, making, 62
Petrol pipe, air-lock in, 49
—— ——, choked, 49

INDEX

Petrol tank, choked air vent, 49
——, water in, 55
Pillion riding, 41
Pinking, 37
Pipe, petrol, choked, 49
Piston, aluminium, 75
—— broken, 48
—— ring gaps, position of, 54
—— rings, removing, 60
Plug points, adjusting, 73
——, reach of, 73
——, sooted, 51
——, sparking, cleaning, 72
Police traps, 94
" Popular " Raleigh, 1
Preliminaries, 26
Preparations for a run, 32
Pump, auxiliary oil, 22
Punctures, 44

RALEIGH clubs, 31
—— depots, 114
—— models, 1-10
—— spare parts stockists, 105-114
Range of Raleigh engines, 12
Rear wheel removal, 45
Reassembling, 62
Re-enamelling, 74
Registration, 27
Reliability trials, 79
Repairs, 44
Reverse, when it must be fitted, 93
Riding, 35
Right, turning to, 39
Rings, piston, removing and examining, 57
Road, prohibited sign, 95
——, proper side of, 41
——, rules of, 41
Roadside repairs, 44
Road signs, 95
——, unattended animals on, 42
Rocker arm sticking, 51
Routes, 84
Royal Automobile Club, 31
Rules of road, 41
Running-in, 37

SADDLE, 24
Second-hand mount, buying, 97

Second-hand mount, selling, 99
Semi-sports model, 3
Shields, leg, 83
Shock absorber, 19
Sidecar, aligning, 73
—— alignment, effect on tyres, 73
—— outfit driving, 38
—— outfit, making left-hand turn with, 38
Sign, dangerous corner, 95
——, " Road Prohibited," 95
——, speed limit, 95
Silencer, explosions in, 55
——, why used, 24
Skids and tramlines, 42
Sooted plugs, 51
Spare parts stockists, 105
Spares, petrol tin, 83
Sparking plug, cleaning, 72
—— —— points, adjusting, 73
—— plugs, reach of, 73
—— ——, sooted, 51
Speed limit, 94
—— ——, sign, 94
Speeds, equivalent, 101
Speedwork, 75
Sports models, 5, 6
Springing, 22
Spring forks, adjusting and lubricating, 67
Starting the engine, 35
Steering and sidecar alignment, 72
—— head, adjusting and oiling, 67
Stockists, Raleigh, 105
Stop, order to, 92
Stopping in traffic, 41
Sturmey-Archer gear-box, 18
Summons, time limit for service, 94

TABLES—
 Engine revolutions, 102
 Formulae for h.p., 102
 Gradients, 101
 Lighting-up times, 103
 Speeds, equivalent, 101
 Tyre size equivalents, 102
Tanks, filling, 32

INDEX

Tappet clearance, adjusting, 53
Tax, 10
Three-speed countershaft gear, 18
Time-table, lighting up, 103
Timing gear, 64
—— magneto, 64
—— the valves, 64
Tour, planning, 80
Touring, 80
—— abroad, 85
Tracing troubles, 46
Traffic, driving in, 41
——, stopping in, 41
Tramcars, passing, 41
Transmission, 19
Trial riding, 77
Troubles, 46
Turning to right or left, 39
Two-stroke engines, 12
Types of engines, 12

Types of machines, 1
Tyre sizes, equivalent, 102
Tyres and sidecar alignment, 72
——, care of, 38
——, pressure of, 38

VALVE, broken, 47
—— bounce, 75
—— clearance, 53
—— grinding, 57
—— spring, 47
—— —— renewal, 61
—— sticking, 55
—— timing, 18, 48, 64

WASHERS, paper making, 62
Water in petrol, 55
Weight of machines, 10
Wheel, detachable, 45
Wind resistance, 78

AUTOBOOKS WORKSHOP MANUALS

ALFA ROMEO GIULIA 1300, 1600, 1750, 2000 1962-1978 WSM
BMW 1600 1966-1973 WSM
BMW 2500, 2800, 3.0 & 3.3 1968-1977 WSM
BMW 316, 320, 320i 1975-1977 WSM
BMW 518, 520, 520i 1973-1981 WSM
FIAT 1100, 1100D, 1100R & 1200 1957-1969 WSM
FIAT 124 1966-1974 WSM
FIAT 124 SPORT 1966-1975 WSM
FIAT 125 & 125 SPECIAL 1967-1973 WSM
FIAT 126, 126L, 126 DV, 126/650 & 126/650 DV 1972-1982 WSM
FIAT 127 SALOON, SPECIAL & SPORT, 900, 1050 1971-1981 WSM
FIAT 128 1969-1982 WSM
FIAT 1300, 1500 1961-1967 WSM
FIAT 131 MIRAFIORI 1975-1982 WSM
FIAT 132 1972-1982 WSM
FIAT 500 1957-1973 WSM
FIAT 600, 600D & MULTIPLA 1955-1969 WSM
FIAT 850 1964-1972 WSM
JAGUAR MK 1, 2 1955-1969 WSM
JAGUAR S TYPE, 420 1963-1968 WSM
JAGUAR XK 120, 140, 150 MK 7, 8, 9 1948-1961 WSM
LAND ROVER 1, 2 1948-1961 WSM
MERCEDES-BENZ 190 1959-1968 WSM
MERCEDES-BENZ 220/8 1968-1972 WSM
MERCEDES-BENZ 220B 1959-1965 WSM
MERCEDES-BENZ 230 1963-1968 WSM
MERCEDES-BENZ 250 1968-1972 WSM
MERCEDES-BENZ 280 1968-1972 WSM
MINI 1959-1980 WSM
MORRIS MINOR 1952-1971 WSM
PEUGEOT 404 1960-1975 WSM
PORSCHE 911 1964-1973 WSM
PORSCHE 911 1970-1977 WSM
RENAULT 16 1965-1979 WSM
RENAULT 8, 10, 1100 1962-1971 WSM
ROVER 3500, 3500S 1968-1976 WSM
SUNBEAM RAPIER, ALPINE 1955-1965 WSM
TRIUMPH SPITFIRE, GT6, VITESSE 1962-1968 WSM
TRIUMPH TR4, TR4A 1961-1967 WSM
VOLKSWAGEN BEETLE 1968-1977 WSM

VELOCEPRESS AUTOMOBILE BOOKS & MANUALS

ABARTH BUYERS GUIDE
AUSTIN-HEALEY 6-CYLINDER WSM
AUSTIN-HEALEY SPRITE & MG MIDGET 1958-1971 WSM
BMW 600 LIMOUSINE FACTORY WSM
BMW 600 LIMOUSINE OWNERS HAND BOOK & SERVICE MANUAL
BMW 2000 & 2002 1966-1976 WSM
BMW ISETTA FACTORY WSM
BOOK OF THE CARRERA PANAMERICANA - MEXICAN ROAD RACE
COMPLETE CATALOG OF JAPANESE MOTOR VEHICLES
CORVAIR 1960-1969 OWNERS WORKSHOP MANUAL
CORVETTE V8 1955-1962 OWNERS WORKSHOP MANUAL
DIALED IN - THE JAN OPPERMAN STORY
FERRARI 250/GT SERVICE AND MAINTENANCE
FERRARI 308 SERIES BUYER'S AND OWNER'S GUIDE
FERRARI BERLINETTA LUSSO
FERRARI BROCHURES AND SALES LITERATURE 1946-1967
FERRARI BROCHURES AND SALES LITERATURE 1968-1989
FERRARI GUIDE TO PERFORMANCE
FERRARI OPP, MAINTENANCE & SERVICE H/BOOKS 1948-1963
FERRARI OWNER'S HANDBOOK
FERRARI SERIAL NUMBERS PART I - ODD NUMBERS TO 21399
FERRARI SERIAL NUMBERS PART II - EVEN NUMBERS TO 1050
FERRARI SPYDER CALIFORNIA
FERRARI TUNING TIPS & MAINTENANCE TECHNIQUES
HENRY'S FABULOUS MODEL "A" FORD
HOW TO BUILD A FIBERGLASS CAR
HOW TO BUILD A RACING CAR
HOW TO RESTORE THE MODEL 'A' FORD
IF HEMINGWAY HAD WRITTEN A RACING NOVEL
JAGUAR E-TYPE 3.8 & 4.2 WSM
LE MANS 24 (THE BOOK THAT THE FILM WAS BASED ON)
MASERATI BROCHURES AND SALES LITERATURE
MASERATI OWNER'S HANDBOOK
METROPOLITAN FACTORY WSM
MGA & MGB OWNERS HANDBOOK & WSM
MG MIDGET TC, TD, TF & TF1500 WORKSHOP MANUAL
OBERT'S FIAT GUIDE
PERFORMANCE TUNING THE SUNBEAM TIGER
PORSCHE 356 1948-1965 WSM
PORSCHE 912 WSM
SOUPING THE VOLKSWAGEN
SOLEX CARBURETORS (EMPHASIS ON UK & EU AUTOMOBILES)
SU CARBURETORS (EMPHASIS ON UK AUTOMOBILES)
TRIUMPH TR2, TR3, TR4 1953-1965 WSM
TUNING FOR SPEED (P.E. IRVING)
VEDA ORR'S NEW REVISED HOT ROD PICTORIAL
VOLKSWAGEN TRANSPORTER, TRUCKS, STATION WAGONS WSM
VOLVO 1944-1968 ALL MODELS WSM
WEBER CARBURETORS (EMPHASIS ON ALFA & FIAT)

BROOKLANDS BOOKS & ROAD TEST PORTFOLIOS (RTP)

AC CARS 1904-2009
ALFA ROMEO 1920-1933 ROAD TEST PORTFOLIO
ALFA ROMEO 1934-1940 ROAD TEST PORTFOLIO
BRABHAM RALT HONDA THE RON TAURANAC STORY
BUGATTI TYPE 10 TO TYPE 40 ROAD TEST PORTFOLIO
BUGATTI TYPE 10 TO TYPE 251 ROAD TEST PORTFOLIO
BUGATTI TYPE 41 TO TYPE 55 ROAD TEST PORTFOLIO
BUGATTI TYPE 57 TO TYPE 251 ROAD TEST PORTFOLIO
DELAHAYE ROAD TEST PORTFOLIO
FERRARI ROAD CARS 1946-1956 ROAD TEST PORTFOLIO
FIAT 500 1936-1972 ROAD TEST PORTFOLIO
FIAT DINO ROAD TEST PORTFOLIO
HISPANO SUIZA ROAD TEST PORTFOLIO
HONDA ST1100/ST1300 PAN EUROPEAN 1990-2002 RTP
JAGUAR MK1 & MK2 ROAD TEST PORTFOLIO
LOTUS CORTINA ROAD TEST PORTFOLIO
MV AGUSTA F4 750 & 1000 1997-2007 ROAD TEST PORTFOLIO
TATRA CARS ROAD TEST PORTFOLIO

VELOCEPRESS MOTORCYCLE BOOKS & MANUALS

AJS SINGLES & TWINS 250cc THRU 1000cc 1932-1948 (BOOK OF)
AJS SINGLES 1955-65 350cc & 500cc (BOOK OF)
AJS SINGLES 1945-60 350cc & 500cc MODELS 16 & 18 (BOOK OF)
ARIEL 1939-1960 4 STROKE SINGLES (BOOK OF)
ARIEL LEADER & ARROW 1958-1964 (BOOK OF)
ARIEL MOTORCYCLES 1933-1951 WSM
ARIEL PREWAR MODELS 1932-1939 (BOOK OF)
BMW M/CYCLES R26 R27 (1956-1967) FACTORY WSM
BMW M/CYCLES R50 R50S R60 R69S (1955-1969) FACTORY WSM
BSA BANTAM ALL MODELS FROM 1948 ONWARDS (BOOK OF)
BSA SINGLES & V-TWINS UP TO 1927 (BOOK OF)
BSA SINGLES & V-TWINS 1936-1939 (BOOK OF)
BSA SINGLES & V-TWINS 1936-1952 (BOOK OF)
BSA OHV & SV SINGLES 250-600cc 1945-1954 (BOOK OF)
BSA OHV & SV SINGLES - 250cc 1954-1970 (BOOK OF)
BSA OHV SINGLES 350 & 500cc 1955-1967 (BOOK OF)
BSA TWINS 1948-1962 (BOOK OF)
BSA TWINS 1962-1969 (SECOND BOOK OF)
CATALOG OF BRITISH MOTORCYCLES (1951 MODELS)
DOUGLAS PRE-WAR ALL MODELS 1929-1939 (BOOK OF)
DOUGLAS POST-WAR ALL MODELS 1948-1957 FACTORY WSM
DUCATI 160cc, 250cc & 350cc OHC MODELS FACTORY WSM
HONDA 50 ALL MODELS UP TO 1970 INC MONKEY & TRAIL (BOOK OF)
HONDA 90 ALL MODELS UP TO 1966 (BOOK OF)
HONDA MOTORCYCLES 125-150 TWINS C/CS/CB/CA WSM
HONDA MOTORCYCLES 250-305 TWINS C/CS/CB WSM
HONDA MOTORCYCLES C100 SUPER CUB WSM
HONDA MOTORCYCLES C110 SPORT CUB 1962-1969 WSM
HONDA TWINS & SINGLES 50cc THRU 305cc 1960-1966 (BOOK OF)
HONDA TWINS ALL MODELS 125cc THRU 450cc UP TO 1968 (BOOK OF)
INDIAN PONYBIKE, BOY RACER & PAPOOSE ILL PARTS LIST & SALES LIT
J.A.P. ENGINES 1927-1952 & MOTORCYCLES 1934-1952 (BOOK OF)
LAMBRETTA ALL 125 & 150cc MODELS 1947-1957 (BOOK OF)
LAMBRETTA LI & TV MODELS 1957-1970 (SECOND BOOK OF)
MATCHLESS 350 & 500cc SINGLES 1945-1956 (BOOK OF)
MATCHLESS 350 & 500cc SINGLES 1955-1966 (BOOK OF)
MOTORCYCLE ENGINEERING (P. E. Irving)
NORTON 1932-1947 (BOOK OF)
NORTON 1938-1956 (BOOK OF)
NORTON DOMINATOR TWINS 1955-1965 (BOOK OF)
NORTON MODELS 19, 50 & ES2 1955-1963 (BOOK OF)
NORTON MOTORCYCLES 1957-1970 FACTORY WSM
NORTON PREWAR MODELS 1932-1939 (BOOK OF)
NSU PRIMA ALL MODELS 1956-1964 (BOOK OF)
NSU QUICKLY ALL MODELS 1953-1963 (BOOK OF)
RALEIGH MOPEDS 1960-1969 (BOOK OF)
RALEIGH MOTORCYCLES 1919-1933 (BOOK OF)
ROYAL ENFIELD SINGLES & V TWINS 1934-1946 (BOOK OF)
ROYAL ENFIELD SINGLES & V TWINS 1937-1953 (BOOK OF)
ROYAL ENFIELD SINGLES 1946-1962 (BOOK OF)
ROYAL ENFIELD 736cc INTERCEPTOR FACTORY WSM
ROYAL ENFIELD 250cc & 350cc SINGLES 1958-1966 (SECOND BOOK OF)
SPEED AND HOW TO OBTAIN IT
SUNBEAM MOTORCYCLES 1928-1939 (BOOK OF)
SUNBEAM S7 & S8 1946-1957 (BOOK OF)
SUZUKI 50cc & 80cc UP TO 1966 (BOOK OF)
SUZUKI T10 1963-1967 FACTORY WSM
SUZUKI T20 & T200 1965-1969 FACTORY WSM
TRIUMPH PRE-WAR MOTORCYCLE 1935-1939 (BOOK OF)
TRIUMPH MOTORCYCLES 1935-1949 (BOOK OF)
TRIUMPH MOTORCYCLES 1937-1951 WSM
TRIUMPH MOTORCYCLES 1945-1955 FACTORY WSM
TRIUMPH TWINS 1945-1958 (BOOK OF)
TRIUMPH TWINS 1956-1969 (BOOK OF)
VELOCETTE ALL SINGLES & TWINS 1925-1970 (BOOK OF)
VESPA 1951-1961 (BOOK OF)
VESPA 125 & 150cc & GS MODELS 1955-1963 (SECOND BOOK OF)
VESPA 90, 125 & 150cc 1963-1972 (THIRD BOOK OF)
VESPA GS & SS 1955-1968 (BOOK OF)
VILLIERS ENGINE (BOOK OF)
VINCENT MOTORCYCLES 1935-1955 WSM

PLEASE VISIT OUR WEBSITE
www.VelocePress.com
**FOR A DETAILED DESCRIPTION
OF ANY OF THESE TITLES**

Please check our website:

www.VelocePress.com

for a complete up-to-date list of available titles

www.ingramcontent.com/pod-product-compliance
Lightning Source LLC
Chambersburg PA
CBHW070552170426
43201CB00012B/1817